DYSFUNCTION
IN THE NAME OF JESUS

Confronting the Idol of Pastoral Workaholism

JAMES ELLIS III, EDITOR

Also by James Ellis III

An Inward-Outward Witness
Suffering's Role in Forming Faithful Preachers

Tell the Truth, Shame the Devil
Stories about the Challenges of Young Pastors

Advance Praise for *Dysfunction in the Name of Jesus*

At the risk of adding another task to your already lengthy list of things you feel you need to achieve, I recommend setting aside a morning (or longer) to sit with the reflections of these wise and experienced ministry leaders. You won't necessarily find a new set of practices to replace the old dysfunctional ones, but you will find wisdom and encouragement from some good people who have been there, and that might just be enough for now.

—Kenton C. Anderson
President of Providence University College
and Theological Seminary
Author of *Theological Education* (Kregel 2024)
and *Integrative Preaching* (Baker Academic 2018)

James Ellis assembles a symphony of authors to help preachers drown out the cacophony of ministerial distractions, not the least of which is workaholism. The melodious themes composed in this book provide insightful correctives for any workaholic preacher. The chapter tunes are sweet reminders of the way it should be and can be in ministry as we deal with the siren call of the idol of workaholism.

—Scott M. Gibson
David E. Garland Chair of Preaching and
Director of the PhD Program in Preaching
George W. Truett Theological Seminary
Baylor University

Smyth & Helwys Publishing
6316 Peake Road
Macon, Georgia 31210-3960
1-800-747-3016
©2025 by James Ellis III
All rights reserved.

Library of Congress Cataloging-in-Publication Data

Names: Ellis, James, III, editor.
Title: Dysfunction in the name of Jesus : confronting the idol of pastoral
workaholism / edited by James Ellis III.
Description: 1st. | Macon, GA : Smyth & Helwys Publishing, [2024] |
Includes bibliographical references.
Identifiers: LCCN 2024039420 | ISBN 9781641735797 (paperback)
Subjects: LCSH: Clergy--Mental health. | Clergy--Job stress. | Burn out
(Psychology)--Religious aspects--Christianity. | Pastoral theology.
Classification: LCC BV4398 .D97 2024 | DDC 253/.2--dc23/eng/20240926
LC record available at https://lccn.loc.gov/2024039420

Disclaimer of Liability: With respect to statements of opinion or fact available in this work of nonfiction, Smyth & Helwys Publishing, nor any of its employees, makes any warranty, express or implied, or assumes any legal liability or responsibility for the accuracy or completeness of any information disclosed, or represents that its use would not infringe privately-owned rights.

Dedication

To fellow pastors who can appreciate this nameless insight: "No one ever said on their deathbed, 'I wish I would have spent more time at work.'" Remember, "man does not live on bread alone, but on every word that comes from the mouth of the Lord" (Deut 8:3). Love what you do, but be resolute about not being defined by it. Love what you do, but love even more the One who called you to do it and sustains you in it. Your work has its place, but as a beloved child of God, learn that being in His presence, *first* and *most often*, yields rich, eternal dividends. Moving at "ludicrous speed" (as depicted in the 1987 film *Spaceballs* with Rick Moranis and John Candy) is not a badge of honor issued by the Spirit. I hope you find lifelong friendships saturated with joy, truth, and grace, and embrace the magnificent sobriety of teaching people how to treat you—even employers, even churches. Saying "No" is a complete sentence. Do not recant or explain it again and again until it means nothing. Be wise, be reasonable, but stand firm.

To my parents, James and Bonnie Ellis, Jr.—through hard work and beautiful sacrifices, you demonstrated the consequence of self-worth, boundary-setting, and valuing family, which has helped me keep my vocation in its proper place.
Thank you.

To Renata, my dear wife—there are no divinely premade worker bees in the kingdom, sentenced to a life of sweat, assembly line productivity, worry, and fatigue. It is stroke of genius, obedience, or both to rest, vacation, smell flowers, and move at a slower pace for the love of God.
I love you dearly!

Contents

Acknowledgments ... ix
Foreword *(Corné J. Bekker)* ... xiii
Foreword *(Kirk Byron Jones)* ... xvii
Editor's Note ... xix

Chapter 1
Making the Best of a Day Off ... 1
  (Karen Stiller)

Chapter 2
Grumbling People-pleasing, and God's Grace ... 9
  (Jim Samra)

Chapter 3
"What You Are Doing Is Not Good": ... 17
Exodus 18 and Pastoral Overwork
  (Steven S. Tuell)

Chapter 4
Winded Prophet ... 27
  (Bryan Dunagan)

Chapter 5
How "Inefficiency" with God Prevents Pastoral Burnout ... 35
  (Micah Lang)

Chapter 6
Clergy Burnout, the Spirit's Fire, and Preaching ... 45
  (Michael Pasquarello III)

Chapter 7
Comfort-curated Ministry 53
  (Dave Dack)

Chapter 8
The Work of Rest 63
  (Stephen L. Woodworth)

Chapter 9
Confronting the Myth of the Balanced Life 73
  (Jul Medenblik)

Chapter 10
Confessions of a Recovering Workaholic 81
  (Rob A. Culbertson)

Chapter 11
Time Alone: Discovering My Identity 89
  (David Sherbino)

Chapter 12
Turning Down the Volume on Demands 99
  (Kyle Denny)

Acknowledgments

When I was working on my first book (of poetry, published in 2004, that is now out of print), I told God that, regardless of whether people bought what I wrote, if He continued opening doors, I would keep at it. To date, nothing I have authored has sold like hotcakes. I am a small-time pastor-scholar, and my research areas do not reflect what is typically featured in *USA Today*, *The New York Times*, or the popular sections of Christian nonfiction. So be it. I simply want to do my part and trust God to do the heavy lifting. He will accomplish His will with my humble musings, and He alone deserves the glory for this and any other manuscripts of mine that reach publication.

I hope something in this collection helps people break free from the manic tremors of overwork. For pastors and anyone else—especially those in the "help professions"—it might seem like a minor issue that working oneself to the bone is a natural consequence of devotion to upstanding causes, but believe me, it is not! However, I do not have the pastoral life all figured out; far from it. In fact, figuring it all out is not my goal. I am a work in progress each day, under construction by the Holy Spirit. With each birthday celebrated, I gain clarity about who I do not want to become as a pastor and about the key values that inspire and instruct me most. Jesus is the standard. We follow His actions, words, and heart, adjusting to the sanctifying rhythms of holiness. We steward ministry in His name, for His sake, and in His power.

He also provides us with those whose example nudges us in the right direction. For me, pastors like Andy Davis, Emmanuel L. McCall, Sr., Rock Dillaman, Robert Smith, Jr., David Renwick, Jim Melson, and the late Bryan Dunagan (1979-2023), who has an essay to this book, fit the bill. They have all faced triumphs and difficulties regarding ministry work and its invasive demands. This book would not have materialized without the support and understanding they provided me through the years. I wholeheartedly believe in working hard, but not in a disturbed manner—and certainly not unto death in the name of ministry. It pains me that biblical expositors and shepherds entrusted with leading people into lives of truth and devotion would twist things to suggest that burnout is not that bad, especially considering the undeniable relational, physical, spiritual, and emotional ruin it brings.

As a child, I watched my parents, striving for their slice of middle-class steadiness, sacrifice to secure opportunities for my sister and me—opportunities they did not have for one reason or another. It was a true parental thing to do that I try not to take for granted. I never saw them as bitter about it—just serious and responsible, sometimes in ways that felt too weighty when they instilled those ethics in us. In due time, I not only survived but came into my own, benefiting from the possibilities that they chose to forgo provided me. And from a household where Jesus was not a confessed or invited presence in our daily lives, I met him as a distracted college student and surrendered to His call, which is a miracle as far as I am concerned.

My father enlisted right out of high school and spent two and a half decades in the U.S. Air Force, only to retire a second time after more years of service as a civilian contractor. My mother, who ultimately worked as a bank teller as we got older, shepherded the home and us kids as her proud vocation for most of my childhood. They have been married for 50 years. Their sense of "had to" and mine are not the same, but I am indebted to them for the foundation they gave me, which helps me guard against turning ministry into something God never intended. Although convictional integrity on this issue has cost me—as it often does—I resolved long ago to take those losses on the chin. It is not my job to manage others' insecurities or immaturities. If you want a pastor who is steadfast about giving his last drop of blood to the church as a martyr-like figure, then we are misaligned. Unless the Lord says otherwise (and he certainly has the right to do so), it is best for us to love one another from a distance.

I currently serve a great church of industrious retirees. Their beautiful building once hosted close to 500 worshippers each week, with all manner of weekday programming and half their budget going to global missions. These days, with about 25 people in worship most Sundays, I tell them all the time that we are "small but mighty." As I serve and lead them through post-pandemic discernment, deciding whether to pivot again to keep the doors open or to close with dignity, I want to acknowledge the kind, loving support system they are to me. This little church, Maplewood Reformed, has valued my non-anxious presence, which is one of the first times in my career that this has happened. They know I take a long nap on Sundays once returning from church. While I am considerably proactive and present as their pastor, they understand I am not available for everything, 24/7/365. They know that I have a life outside of ministry, that my wife comes first, and that I work hard to ensure my world does not revolve entirely around pastoral work. We are not perfect, but they seem to genuinely want me to pursue overall health rather than running on the fumes of fatigue or idolatry.

Trust me, the pains of numerical decline do not often lead to flexibility or graceful behavior—especially (unfortunately) in church. The Lord knows that cooperation often goes out the window. If anything, people double down on scarcity, control, and selfishness. We fight over the smallest, most insignificant things, convinced that we can save ourselves with the shiniest idea or the right person. In times of abundance or struggle, I do not want to be like that, and it means the world that this church has championed a bald, non-Calvinist (ordained in the Baptist tradition), introverted pastor with tattoos to walk with them. I cannot predict the future of Maplewood after its 83 years of ministry, nor the future of churches facing similar variables. But I am confident that trusting God enough to conform to His ways is the best course of action.

—James

Foreword

The twenty-first century is a confusing time for ministers. Late modernity, coupled with the opportunities and demands of the digital age, has created a perfect storm of identity confusion for clergy. The growing demands of contemporary ministry mean that church leaders must lead like expert organizational chief officers, managing churches by adopting every novel business tool while attempting to break through social media's cacophony with the gospel's eternal message. The age-old and classical duties of the pastor, devotion to prayer and the ministry of the word (Acts 6:4), have been augmented to include expectations of being a community leader, organizational manager, mental health counselor, digital influencer, public thought leader, and many more roles as the ecclesial and societal landscapes change. Trying to fulfill these unceasing demands in a secularized context can be exhausting and ultimately debilitating. It is no surprise that many pastors report experiences of vocational unhappiness, depression, and even burnout. The quest to be all for everyone becomes an endless chase in a small place. In this impossible quest for perfection, the practice of ministerial overwork becomes normative, and with it come eventual leadership failures. Is there another way?

The reasons for ministerial role confusion, imbalance, and overwork are myriad and complex. The quest to understand and address the erosion of ministerial health should include wide-ranging inquiries guided by the word of God and the great faithful tradition. We would also do well to follow the wisdom of Proverbs and remember that in "an abundance of counselors there is safety" (Prov 11:14, ESV). We should widen the conversation to learn from all the wealth of the church, noting its rich experiences and wisdom in the Majority World. In the quest for an ecclesial reset, theological understandings of the nature and function of the church and her witness in the world must be biblically revisited, reclaimed, and respected. Likewise, a renewal of a thoroughly faithful theology of ministry can offer a remedy to this pastoral instability. Only a robust, biblical theology and praxis of church and ministry can stem the devastating tide of ministerial self-sabotage.

The ever-present danger of workaholism finds its most troubling expression in turning ministry into an idol. However, this occurs only when we forget whom we are serving. Ministers are, first and foremost, God's servants. We only serve others as an expression of service to God. The fourth-century church father John Chrysostom, in his commentary on St. John, the Apostle and Evangelist, reminds us of this grounding reality (Homily 3):

> A servant performs all he does for the pleasure of his master and seeks nothing more than his approving glance; he does not draw the eyes of others to his work, even if these others are great, but regards one thing only; how the master regards his work. Is it not strange, then, that we who have such a Master, seek for another audience, who by their gazing can give us no aid, but instead, harm us and rob of merit all our toil?

Chrysostom roots this theology of ministry in the biblical description of a minister as a servant. The Apostle Paul, in the "Carmen Christi" (Hymn to Christ) recorded in his letter to the Philippians, admonishes us to "have this mind among yourselves, which is yours in Christ Jesus, who, though he was in the form of God, did not count equality with God a thing to be grasped, but emptied himself, by taking the form of a servant, being born in the likeness of men" (Phil 2:5-7, ESV). The Pauline description of a Christ follower as a servant is easily misunderstood as an encouragement to the boundary-less work we see among those afflicted with ministerial workaholism. However, when we consider the one whom these servants serve, Christ Jesus, balance and health are restored. Remembering Christ is paramount.

Jesus described the nature of his call to service when he said, "Come to me, all who labor and are heavy laden, and I will give you rest. Take my yoke upon you, and learn from me, for I am gentle and lowly in heart, and you will find rest for your souls. For my yoke is easy, and my burden is light" (Matt 11:28-30, ESV). Christ calls ministers to balanced and healthy service. It is a humble call to service marked by gentleness, rest, and a light and easy burden.

May this much-needed volume draw us back to the feet of the one we are called to serve, who first loved us. May our worldly and carnal ideas of ministry and church fall to the side. May we discover that the one we serve is the one who calls us into rest and joy. May our hearts be healed from the misguided efforts to confer sullied ideas of joy and purpose. May we find our home in Christ, his presence, and gentle service. Come, Lord Jesus, help and heal your church. Come, Lord Jesus, come!

—Corné J. Bekker, DLitt. et Phil.
Regent University School of Divinity
Virginia Beach, Virginia

Foreword

No Other Reason

*Savor a
long moment
of feeling graced
and accepted
for no other reason
than just that
you are.*

I had not planned to begin this foreword with poetry. The words are my own, having come to mind recently at the beginning of my morning devotion. I felt unusually burdened that morning, not so much by anything wrong but by taking account of more than fifty years spent preaching, forty years pastoring, and thirty years teaching in seminaries and writing and editing books. Remembering has become an unscheduled pastime on the eve of retirement (better yet, re-wirement) in just a few months.

It's been quite a marathon, and I feel blessed beyond words to have made it more than well enough, if scarred, through it all.

Making it well in ministry, through it all, is what you will read about in this good book. Making it well is more daunting than before but is doable with eyes, heart, mind, and soul wide open to exploration, wisdom, and change. Look for these signs as you read, and take the crucial step of integrating what resonates with how you live and work. Do so with clarity and intention.

You must be open to something else. More than anything, be open to the opportunity.

*of feeling graced
and accepted
for no other reason
than just that you are.*

Along with learning strategies to prevent the crushing, debilitating, overloaded, hurried existence that ministry can become, you may choose to receive God's limitless grace and acceptance that have nothing to do with the call on your life.

Yet heeding the first and lasting call to God's gracious, precious love supplies insurmountable inspiration for the impossible job of ministry. Much wisdom will serve you well and help you not just survive ministry but thrive in it. And an abiding sense of divine acceptance unrelated to anything you do will make such wild and wonderful thriving on dangerous terrain lighter and lovelier.

—Kirk Byron Jones, PhD, DMin
Zion Baptist Church
Lynn, Massachusetts

Editor's Note

"If you don't take good care of yourself, who will?" Those in ministry, in whatever capacity, cannot afford to avoid this question. After taking it head on, you should prayerfully, practically, and powerfully take grownup steps to safeguard yourself and yours from falling apart. Run away as fast as possible from anyone trying to convince you that burning out or upholding unhealthy expectations (your own or from others) is a rite of passage. They are not. Hazing and ministry do not go together.

I agree that pastors can be lazy, so we can get that out of the way from the start. Being redeemed by Jesus's shed blood and called to serve him, and then uniquely caring for his people as an undershepherd is cool. Still, as with everybody else, sin remains a thick sludge within those who preach and teach until we return to the ground, "earth to earth, ashes to ashes, dust to dust." Some ministers fudge their hours or play video games when they should be visiting the sick and preparing sermons. Pastors do not fundamentally have hearts of gold. Sadly, enough of them have a slothful work ethic. Some are more excited about displaying academic degrees on the wall, brewing homemade beer in their basement, or thirstily chasing influencer status than they are about corralling, correcting, and caring for God's sheep and leading people to Christ. Should someone compile essays addressing any of these *acedia*, I would gladly contribute. But this book is about correctly identifying pastoral workaholism as an idol so we can be better equipped to contend against it for the sake of Christ, with the Spirit's help.

A few days ago, in January, my small town—situated on the edge of Lake Michigan—was hit by a brutal winter storm. We have heated sidewalks downtown to encourage tourism during these times, but that did not stop the several feet of fluffy, icy snow that fell along with arctic temperatures. One morning, it dropped to -4°F, and with the wind chill, it felt like -25°F. Let that sink in. In our 1946 bungalow, the city's main water supply pipes were so offended by the cold that they froze solid. That meant a hasty retreat to a hotel for three days, waiting for the temperature to creep up into the teens and twenties. Meanwhile, I kept a space heater running nonstop, aimed directly at the plumbing, hoping to thaw it out. One afternoon, after hours of clearing snow from our sidewalks and driveway and tossing ice melt everywhere, I headed back to the hotel only to pass a truck stuck at the bottom of a driveway. The Ohio driver, who was here innocently checking on his vacation home, seemed to have underestimated the depth of the snow and ice underneath it and overestimated the power of his Dodge Ram 1500 Big Horn. I pulled over, assessed the situation with him, and together we hatched a plan. He tied some boating ropes of his to my SUV to help pull him out. It worked! We chatted for a bit afterward, both feeling like we had accomplished something worthwhile, and he offered to pay me for my time and effort, which I declined. We then went our separate ways.

Anyone who knows me knows that I enjoy helping people. But the significance of this story is this: I am on leave from my church as this incident occurred. Due to the polity of my church's denomination, since I am not ordained in their tradition, my employment must be negotiated on a yearly contract. As my old contract was ending and a new one had been agreed to in principle, I had seven weeks of combined study and vacation leave to use—otherwise, I would need to forfeit it. And since there is nothing in my body or soul that believes in forfeiting compensation, this extended time away became necessary. While I love helping others and do so regularly, it is much harder to lean into these opportunities when you are constantly preparing for funerals, Sunday sermons, meetings, managing staff, and responding to e-mails. It is easy to slip into autopilot, disregarding important moments because they feel trivial compared to ministry's relentless demands. It is debilitating. If pastors, in particular, are so caught up in internal and external chaos—or in a culture of pastoral extremism upheld by their churches—that they neglect the time needed to occasionally lend a stranger a helping hand, be thoughtful, laugh without pretense, sit in silence, or passionately tend to their own overall well-being in other ways, then we have a real problem. And, unfortunately, we do have a problem.

I know pastors who, after 8, 18, or even 28 years of service—many who have been at the same church all that time—have never taken the Sundays or weeks off associated with Easter, Christmas, or Mother's Day. Privately, they speak of feeling like hamsters in a wheel, trapped in a cycle of fealty, to quote the *John Wick* film franchise: "I have served. I will be of service." "I would love to take that time off some years, but my church would freak out," they say. Respectfully, it feels like we, as a collective, are a bunch of cowards or hypocrites. Many of us decry personality-driven ministries that elevate the pastor to godlike status, yet we lead and live as if God's mission and power go ghost when we are not in the pulpit. I know pastors who rarely take vacations, and when they do, they still end up doing church work. Their loved ones and bodies that keep score are not fans of it, even if they try to love them through it. I know pastors who have put their own homes up as collateral to help their churches secure capital expansion loans. I know pastors who stopped taking walks because they are "too busy" and who never seem to have time for their spouses, kids, or even themselves. They think this is the way it must be—moreover, that a special crown awaits them in heaven for it. It is easy for the blind to lead the blind. The trouble starts when you begin to see like the man at Bethsaida in Mark 8:22-26 or Bartimaeus later in Mark 10:46-52. What we need are pastors whose hearts are being renovated, who understand themselves, the Lord, and their calling in a fundamentally improved, more biblically accurate way.

The concept of "workaholism" was first introduced by the pioneering pastor-scholar Wayne Oates in his 1971 book *Confessions of a Workaholic: The Facts about Work Addiction* (World Pub. Co.). However, this issue has existed for as long as pastoral ministry itself, with unrealistic expectations about such work becoming normalized among pastors, parishioners, and even those outside the church. You can see this dynamic reflected in Marianne Bernhard's May 1981 *Washington Post* article, "Clergy Burnout: When Stress and Overwork Overwhelm the Spirit." The theme is also explored in the 1996 film *The Preacher's Wife* (dir. Penny Marshall), starring Denzel Washington and Whitney Houston, as well as its 1947 predecessor, *The Bishop's Wife* (dir. Henry Koster). Novels like *And the Shofar Blew* by Francine Rivers (2003) and the writings of church fathers, monastics, reformers, and other Christian leaders throughout history further illustrate the point. It becomes clear that pastoral leaders have long struggled—and still do, to an even greater extent today—against the temptation to "do too much." This dynamic continues to thrive within these circles and beyond, like a stubborn, insidious weed, trapping clergy in servitude to an obsession that feels larger than life and whose allure is deceptively compelling. After nearly two decades of navigating the pastoral vocation—serving as both a pastor and a college/university chaplain—I can tell you that it makes for an odd, often intense life. The struggle is real.

People often do not understand, and many do not want to. Rightly or wrongly, they have their own lives and worries. They are not concerned with how isolating your work can be or how under-compensated you are—almost as if you took a vow of poverty, which, at least in my case, I did not. They mean well, but not all of them, and not all the time. To some, you are just a tool of the institution their paychecks fund. Whether they tithe or give at all in the first place is another story. You are expected to be at their kid's Barbie-themed birthday party or soccer game, ready to troubleshoot their relationship, health, or spiritual crises, and dispense wisdom like it is a never-ending resource, drawn from a life handcuffed to sermons, Bible studies, counseling sessions, staff development, and congregational leadership. And you are supposed to do all of this in the name of Jesus, every day and all day like a cute, cuddly Energizer Bunny. Because, after all, isn't that what pastors sign up to do? The "concierge" approach to ministry that treats pastors like spiritual Amazon delivery drivers is not from God. I decided long ago that ministry would not be my primary calling, and for that and some other choices, I have faced criticism. You may be labeled many things if you work hard, but still maintain healthy boundaries. Nevertheless, I am grateful that God called me to this unique role, even though it brings its own set of frustrations. I just refuse to let the work define me. It is not worth it. My wife deserves a fully present husband who prioritizes her and our life together, not someone who can only talk about church life at a dinner party, who needs to be needed by the church, or who must be nagged to death to ever take time off. Let me be clear: I love what I do, but I do not need everyone to like me. I want God to be proud of how I seek to honor Him, His people, my wife, and the gifts He entrusted me with.

As an African American, I have served in multiracial, predominantly Anglo, and predominantly African American ecclesial settings. I was born in Japan due to my father's career in the Air Force, while my wife was raised in an Army family that moved frequently. Together, we have lived in ten states and three countries. Only God knows where we might be sent next. It does not make for an easy, predictable, or cushy life. But sacrificing myself on the altar of ministry is foolish and unfaithful. May the exclusivity of Jesus—our sole portion in life and in death—refine you from the inside out. Be mindful of guardrails and guidelines that promote you staying grounded. Pursue holiness as a pastor because God has set the precedent (Lev 11:44-45; 19:2). No superheroes are coming to save you or remedy your disordered ways. God has already done that and continues to do so, often sending loved ones or even strangers to help you along the way. I hope *Dysfunction in the Name of Jesus: Confronting the Idolatry of Pastoral Workaholism* is a balm that the Spirit uses in your life towards that end.

This volume has honestly been a bit of a challenge to compile, although I suppose that comes with the experience. I reached out to pastors, seminary professors, and ministers from all over—through social media, friends of friends, and other networks—with little success, particularly when it came to attaining the level of diversity I had hoped for. But these things happen. Despite the challenges, it is still a worthwhile undertaking, and I am proud of what has been assembled. One recurring refrain I heard from a wide range of pastoral leaders—some well-known, some not—when I asked them to contribute went something like this: "James, this is an important issue, and I would love to submit something. But as ironic as it is, I am just too busy to find the time to write. Sorry. Please let me know when the book is out—I need to read it." This response partly illustrates how overtaxed we are. In life and ministry, balance, prioritization, and mature identities are elusive. No one here is advocating for the kind of unrealistic, utopian thinking that implies everything can float along in perfect equilibrium every moment of every day. I am not complaining about the sacrifices that come with serving people in Jesus' name as a pastor—though voices like Peter Scazzero's, for example, offer both ancient and modern rhythms that can help us work more sensibly and sustainably. I am not suggesting pastors should "quietly quit" or standardize mediocrity or unprofessionalism—the opposite of being responsible. Ministry is a grind, and some of that is just the static reality of the matter. But let us be clear: pastoring is not the "holy grail." It represents meaningful, incarnational work, but so does what is provided by military personnel, first responders, educators, and healthcare and social workers. In one of the courses I teach at Winebrenner Theological Seminary, a student, Henry Volk, reflected: "Fast-food churches preach a QR code Jesus." As prophetic and accurate as his statement is, too many pastors are also living QR code lives—failing to lead by example. We can do better. *Dysfunction in the Name of Jesus* is one step in the larger need for reform.

—James Ellis III, DMin
Maplewood Reformed Church
Winebrenner Theological Seminary
Holland, Michigan

Making the Best of a Day Off

Karen Stiller

Our first parish post was in the Canadian Prairies but so far north that we had left the flat land and golden grasses far behind to the south of us. This was lake and forest and freshwater fishing country, where moose would amble down the sides of narrow highways in their weighty way. From there, it was a long drive to anywhere, past taxidermy shops alternating with truck stops that made huge all-day breakfast platters for low prices, with hungry men in mind. You had to want to leave that town and plan for it. Random ambling was not encouraged. We left almost every Friday that we could, driving almost two hours away, usually to the Boston Pizza in the closest city, which was in the next province over. Friday was the pastor's day off. And to get a true day off, we left town. Brent was the rector of the Anglican church, and we lived in the rectory, which was on the main street just down from the cowboy statue and beside the senior's villa. Any excursion within the town could turn pastoral quickly. Send him to the store for garbage bags and you'd lose him for two hours. Staying home on a day off with curtains drawn and the car squeezed into the garage did not solve the problem. If we were in the little bungalow on Centre Street doing chores or reading a book, church people would drop in. After all, it was Brent's day off. What better time for a visit? They didn't know *they* were work. I knew going into this life that a pastor didn't necessarily work regular hours, but I didn't realize that they could work all the waking hours if they let themselves or could not stop themselves.

This vocation seeps through everything. If there are walls, they are usually soft and permeable and can barely stand under the pressure. The most modest of boundaries pastors hope to build, like regular days off, predictable office hours, and uninterrupted vacations, can collapse easily under the weight. The goodness of the work—and so much is good—can flow and grow and spill out over everything else, like a sink overflowing all over the kitchen floor. Pastors must be careful. It takes a lot of work not to overwork.

This is especially true in the beginning, when it can feel like you are creating things out of dust and dreams, with paper and glue. You might have to set out the chairs yourselves and then stack them back up again after the worship service. In the beginning, you might be preaching and planning the potluck as well as the picnic next week. There are funerals, fiftieth-anniversary teas, and Vacation Bible School programming, which you and your spouse are running, plus ball games to attend. You are doing new things because the church assured you in your interview that they want to grow and expand and are behind you all the way. Additionally, you are likely doing all the old, other things that will always need to be done. It's probably all hands on deck for your family too, which you try to make as fun as possible whenever you can so they won't notice it's actually a lot of work. Your family loves Jesus, and they love you too, and they want you to succeed at this holy endeavor that you've brought them all into. They are all swept up into it, as if by a big broom.

Every Sunday afternoon, for quite a while, Brent's mother called to ask how things went and to inquire of him how many people were in church that morning. She was an interested mom and didn't mean to add to the pressure, I'm sure, but her question did. Finally, he asked her to stop. The soil of overwork is dark and deep, rich and moist, and so very tempting. Whole churches can grow from it. So can perfectionism, envy and ego, and a belief that you are required for everything. It all starts as a tiny seed that can easily become an oak tree.

When we left that first small town for a bigger church in a large city, it felt like a promotion to me, even though I knew in my heart I wasn't supposed to feel that way about it. It wasn't a holy thought.

But I couldn't help it. There seemed to be a ladder, after all—even if we pretended there wasn't and tried not to think about it—and it felt as if we had hopped up a few rungs with one small leap. One night, in our new, shiny city, we met an old acquaintance from seminary days at a play we attended at a small Christian theater. It was a production of *Narnia* although I can barely remember the lion, the witch, or the wardrobe. What I remember most is the question our friend asked, almost right away, while still shaking Brent's hand: "How many people are in your church?" Brent and I can't remember what he answered, but he's not one to be put into a corner, so he would have murmured something non-definitive, and un-numbery. Plus, by then, we were already a good distance down the road of the Anglican way. There are notable exceptions, but typically these congregations are not big enough to impress your seminary buddies. They tend toward the intimate and candlelit, with hymnbooks that have dedications to grandfathers and old aunties pasted inside the front cover. There are "cradle Anglicans" (often lovely little old ladies who have outlasted seven rectors) and "new Anglicans" (often weary Evangelicals coming to rest a while), but there are not herds or hordes of Anglicans running around anywhere, generally speaking.

Whatever the tradition, it is easy to think that our churches are never quite big enough. We can never work hard enough if we don't figure out how to stop. What I saw in front of me that night, which I have also seen inside of me a lot of days, is the count-by-numbers trap of ministry success. If you sell insurance, maybe the size of your house marks you as a leader in your field. If you own a restaurant, maybe it's the make of your car. If you're a pastor, and you're not careful, it's the size of your church or the number of campuses you administer, spread over counties. This is hard to resist. Bigger just sounds better. Once, we walked through a church building of a congregation that was interviewing Brent, and I thought and almost said out loud, "This building is not big enough." That's how certain I was that Brent would fill it up and overflow it; he was that good at being a pastor. The guy could preach. That church did fill up, and then it emptied a little when the ladies' group turned against him (like an angry mob) after he thwarted an end-of-year tea leaf–reading social evening their hearts were set on. That was also when he started to go gray. If they don't dye their hair—and they shouldn't—pastors are like presidents in how rapidly they go gray upon taking office. Things went up and down from there—better when new families came with energy, and then some people left (not loving all the noisy new families). Brent bringing out his guitar and singing a few praise choruses made a few people skedaddle. Keeping track can be a whirlwind and can end up amounting to just chasing the wind. You can't control what you can't control. Your worth is not determined by the numbers. This is hard for all of us to remember.

You are a chapter in the history of a church, and they are a chapter in yours. Some people will remember you and all your work. Most won't. Pastors can be ambitious because people can be ambitious. The wrong ambitions can steer your ship right into the rocks. Married to the minister, I have fought my own ambition battle, watching a family leave for the bigger and therefore better-to-them church across town, annoyed with my husband for annoying them, if that's what happened. "What now?" I'd sometimes say when the phone rang. Are we doing enough? Being enough? Working enough? The overwork comes naturally to most of us. It is the stopping that is so tough. That is what takes confidence and, most of all, trust. When you're a shepherd running through his field, it's easier to feel productive and consequently vital to people and to Jesus. To stop and have a cup of tea with someone—especially someone unstrategic who is not a mover and a shaker but a quiet, still someone from your church, a single and solitary (maybe really old) sheep—can sometimes be the hardest work. And, of course, whenever we talk about overwork among clergy, someone rightfully points out that even Jesus took time apart and resisted the adoration of the crowds. Pastors know that already. They've heard it a thousand times. You can lead a pastor to that still water, but it takes a lot of work before they will drink it. To stop and sit is to trust. To retreat is to repent. To serve quietly and be content with the enough of it all is our holy quest.

If you're a shepherd who has a wife, I want to share something difficult. There are private Facebook groups for women married to pastors, created by other women married to pastors, and we are talking about you in there. If there's a Facebook group for men who are married to pastors, I can only assume the conversation is similar.

One group has a sweet rule that we can't post videos of our husbands preaching their sermons. Just imagine all the wives posting clips of their husbands preaching for all the other women to watch. Not all the talk is negative, and some of it is so pleased and proud that it's borderline boastful. We do love you so. But when you're fabulous at church and a bit of a jerk at home, probably because of your overwork and undertrust, this is noticed and noted. Advice is sought and dispensed with precision: "This is what I did when he did that." "This is what you should tell him." "Don't let him get away with that." Women married to ministers are seeking each other out for prayer and support because no one else really understands this life of overwork rooted in serving God, which makes motivation and healing tough to untangle.

Emergency prayer alerts are sent out when you're so tired that you're sick or so listless that you spend your day off snoring on the couch in the basement instead of doing the things you said you would do. Or when you're so grouchy because your big idea failed, or the youth pastor is acting up again. No one shares names of people or places, but these Facebook conversations have a lot to do with survival. Spouses wonder how long they can sustain the pace of your pace. Maybe it's time to ask your spouse if they are having as much fun as you are. Or as little fun as you are. Things might be different for your partner than they thought it would be, or assumed it would be, when you first set out together. You're definitely gone more than anyone thought you would be and available less than you are probably needed. The people who love you the most and whom you are supposed to be loving the best notice how tired you are, and some of them are asking complete strangers to help sort it out.

"Even the best pastor is not omnicompetent, though he or she might be under considerable pressure to appear so,"[1] writes Craig C. Hill in his helpful book *Servant of All: Status, Ambition, and the Way of Jesus*. Hill was dean of Perkins School of Theology, and he gave all the new seminary students a copy of the book, so pervasive did he find the temptation to scramble for status and achievement among new pastors. "How do we resist?" he writes. "We resist together."² Early Christian communities were small, and their success or failure was measured by the behavior of the converts within these communities, writes Hill, not the prowess of the leader: "They would win or lose together."³ That's a lovely thought. It wasn't all about the pastor. It wasn't all about the giftedness—omnicompetence!—of the leader. I had not heard the word "omnicompetent" before, but I agree. To be highly skilled at all things is a pressure in the ministry life, almost a job requirement in some circles. I would add to that list immensely creative, kind, and gentle but also prophetically truthful and available to come for dinner when invited, charming (in a holy way) but not off-putting, if you know what I mean, and being good-looking is a plus, as is knowing when to leave the wedding reception of the ceremony you officiated at earlier in the day so people can start having more fun.

"I will disappoint you," Brent told every new church when he started as their pastor. By then, I already knew that he was not omnicompetent, but no one else knew for certain, and they probably secretly hoped he would be. I wondered sometimes if he was taking the right approach with that disappointment line, but now, years later, I think it was good and right to say. We are all either the disappointing or the disappointed at various times and in many places. There is no way around it, only with it and through it. We are not omnicompetent. To pretend otherwise is to flirt with ego and disaster and a crushing workload, inviting disappointment all across the board. Another thing Brent would say, which I also didn't like, was, "God doesn't need us." He liked to remind people that we were dispensable in God's big plan. He'd say it matter-of-factly, as if it weren't like having a big bucket of ice poured over your head. It can be unpleasant at first to think that neither glory nor grief, love nor loss, success nor failure hinges on our work or our giftedness. But believing that can help us walk more quietly beside still waters the way we need to. Being willing to be dispensable *and* disappointing must be part of the work of not overworking, of unlocking ourselves from those heavy chains. To own our non-omnicompetence, to invite others into the work as if it really is a team, and to be the right amount of non-indispensable feels like an act of rebellion rooted in good faith. It is to drive a long way out of town on your day off, no matter what you might miss.

Karen Stiller is a writer and author whose husband, Brent (1963–2023), last served as the Rector of St. Peter and St. Paul's Anglican Church in Canada's Ottawa, Ontario. Her latest book is Holiness Here: Searching for God in the Ordinary Events of Everyday Life.

Grumbling, People-pleasing, and God's Grace

Jim Samra

Approximately five and a half years into my tenure as senior pastor, I began hearing rumblings that a secret group was meeting with the goal to get me fired. Sunday mornings, members of this group were bold enough to walk around the back of the sanctuary while I preached, trying to recruit people to join their cause. They gave their group a name, which in its shortened form simply became "The Committee." They circulated petitions demanding my termination and tried to enlist the services of a lawyer. Thankfully, he refused. They even made plans to bring in an outside pastoral consultant to bolster their claims that I was an incompetent pastor. Thankfully, she also refused. Many of them, a group that at some point had grown to a substantial number, outright told the elders they would withhold their giving until their demands were met. On one occasion, one of The Committee's leaders stood at an annual meeting and read a letter he had written denouncing me. They ensnared a member of our pastoral staff to help with the attempted coup and promised him my position if they could get me fired. The most active people working to oust me were longtime members, some of whom had been influential leaders in the church's past. Perhaps of greater disappointment, some were former elders. As a result, the group wasn't simply dismissed as troublemakers but ended up consuming countless hours of time from the current elders who were hesitant to ignore their complaints. For almost two years, The Committee's allegations and injurious behavior hijacked almost every elder meeting and cast a shadow over almost every decision.

I spent more time than anyone else dealing with them. They constantly spread rumors about what I believed, fabricated selfish motives pertaining to any decisions or actions I undertook, and deceived people with false claims about my supposed plans for the church's future. Time and again, I would meet with individuals who were either a part of The Committee or influenced by them. I would listen to their accusations and spend time trying to explain the truth. I assured them I didn't believe what they claimed I did. I showed evidence from my sermons where I had denounced the theological points they seemed so sure I espoused. I pointed out that some of their accusations were mutually exclusive: for example, it was impossible for me to be both a dictator (as they alleged) and powerless in the face of an unruly staff (which they also alleged). My reasoning was in vain. I would spend hours upon hours with someone only to have them leave my office and twist my words to claim the exact opposite of what I had said. Or I would meet individually with confused congregants to reassure them of my intentions only to have to repeat the process after The Committee confused them again, using claims that I had already gone out of my way to disprove, or so I thought. It was exhausting.

Perhaps the worst part of the experience is that one of their major accusations rang true. They accused me of not being a very good pastor, in part because I was not as gracious or merciful as a pastor ought to be. It hit home. This was my first job as the pastor of a church. I hadn't sought the role but rather was thrust into it by God's design. I felt ill-equipped because, well, in certain ways, I was. The opportunity wasn't something I'd been consciously preparing for or seeking out. The job was so overwhelming and the fear of failure so great that I almost quit after the first week. For the first eighteen months as senior pastor, I kept waiting for someone to acknowledge what I felt, that this had been a nice experiment but now we needed to hire a real pastor to lead the church. Despite my protests with God, however, to my surprise, God kept confirming that this was indeed the church he had called me to for this exact position. God kept blessing my efforts.

Despite my fears and failures, he continued showering me with grace. Even as The Committee charged me with being too harsh, I could see the Lord remaking me into a more gracious and merciful person. More than anything, God kept demonstrating to me that his grace was sufficient, and his strength was made perfect in my weaknesses.

Still, in the middle of this crisis with The Committee, I found myself sitting at a table in a library in another part of the country, depleted with feelings of futility and ready to quit. God had kindly arranged for me to be on a short study-leave just after the worst of the crisis hit. I don't know if I would use the term "burnout" for my experience. It was more that I was just plain *done*. I had always thought, or at least hoped, that I would be one of those pastors who made it—who had a long, steady, and faithful career serving God. Sitting there at that table, I realized I probably wasn't going to be one of those pastors. I felt more likely to be a pastor who didn't make it. I had given it my best effort but had come up short. For the first time in my life, I dreaded the idea of going back to the church, the church I had been attending since high school. I didn't even want to go back to the city, my hometown. I wanted to vanish and never return. At that point, I felt a compulsion to open my Bible and read something.

"But I don't want to," I protested. "In fact, I am not sure I ever want to read this again."

"I should read something," I thought. "Isn't the Bible supposed to help at times like this?"

"Where to start, though? Genesis? Not interested in creation right now. Matthew? What good would Jesus's genealogy or the Christmas story be at a time like this?"

Staring blankly at my Bible while these thoughts filled my mind, I noticed that some pages were folded over. Out of habit, I opened the Bible and smoothed them out.

"You could just start here," came the suggestion in my head.

"Why not?" I figured. "What have I got to lose? I have five weeks to kill before I go back and quit my job. I may as well read something from this passage so I can get this over with."

My Bible was open to 1 Samuel 21. I started reading the story of David in the wilderness running from Saul. On that fateful day, it felt like I was seeing the story for the first time. Every detail jumped off the page. I devoured chapter after chapter. It was life for my dry and thirsty soul. I kept going until I reached 2 Samuel 3:1 where we read, "The war between the house of Saul and the house of David lasted a long time. David grew stronger and stronger, while the house of Saul grew weaker and weaker" (NIV). Admittedly, 2 Samuel 3:1 is an innocuous passage. I've never met anyone who claims it as their life verse. I can't even imagine someone hanging it on their fridge for inspiration or memorizing it for reinforcement. But at that point, it came to me as a promise. Though I understood David was the second king in Israel's history, I guess it had never registered that David didn't become king over all of Israel immediately after Saul's death. For the first time, I realized that for seven and a half years, David was only king over part of Israel. The Lord used that passage to speak to my heart and show me that at my church was a "house of Saul" that did not want to accept me as pastor. Second Samuel 3:1 was a boost to me that God was at work. Just as David had been anointed king over Israel but was not yet serving as king over all of Israel, I was selected to be the pastor of the whole church, but God would have to do the work necessary to deal with The Committee, who refused to acknowledge that God had selected me as their pastor.

This was a watershed moment for me. One of the passages that God had used to help me during the senior pastor interview process was 1 Samuel 16, where God selected David to be the next king of Israel without David applying for the job. Similarly, I had been asked as a candidate without ever applying for the job. I was reminded that David didn't look like a king from outward appearance, but God selected him anyway. I may not have looked like a pastor from outward appearance, but God selected me for this role. This connection to David was riveting, so I kept reading. It is easy to forget what a great read 1 and 2 Samuel are, but even more if you see yourself in one of the characters. I was completely drawn into David's story. I kept reading through his triumphs, his failures with Bathsheba and Uriah, and his struggles with Absalom until another part of his story hit me right between the eyes. In 2 Samuel 19–20, David returns to Jerusalem after fleeing from Absalom. Again, in my imagination, I thought all of Israel had welcomed him back with open arms and celebrated the return of the king. But that is not what happened. Many in Israel weren't even sure they wanted him back as king. How could this be? David would go down as the greatest king in Israel's history and a far, far better king than his predecessor . . . and they were not sure if they wanted him back? I was stunned. From there, I sensed the Lord directing me to Moses's story. What stood out to me was all the grumbling, complaining, and downright rebellion that Moses endured from the Israelites, even at one point from his own brother and sister. Here was a man who spoke face to face with God, easily the greatest leader in all of Israel's history, and yet he couldn't please the Israelites.

I then reread the Gospels and was reminded afresh of the stunning truth that despite being the Son of God, despite all the miracles, despite the eternal truth that he taught, despite demonstrating infinite love for us by choosing to become one of us and dying on a cross for us, Jesus couldn't please most people. Through all of this, I heard a stunning accusation from God in my soul: that somehow my emptiness and my feelings of being completely spent in ministry were partly my fault. I couldn't believe what I was hearing. Surely, I was one hundred percent innocent in the situation, a righteous sufferer who deserved nothing but empathy, right? While God categorically denounced the divisiveness, the rebellion, and the rest—which reassured me—God also gently convicted me that part of the problem was that I was a people-pleaser. I protested that I couldn't be a people-pleaser. I was not afraid to tell people difficult things. In fact, one of the accusations leveled against me was that I was not sensitive enough to what people wanted from me.

But God revealed a different aspect of people-pleasing that I was missing. Even though I was willing to say hard things to people, I still wanted them to affirm that I was doing a good job. I wanted them to respect me for working hard and being consistent in my positions even if we came to a different conclusion. I was working myself to death trying to convince them to approve of the job I was doing. And then came the kicker, straight out of Galatians 1:10. I sensed God presenting me with a choice: if The Committee (or anyone in general) was pleased with me, God wouldn't be. The rebuke was as kind as it was accurate. I was chasing an unattainable goal. If people revolted against David, Moses, and even Jesus, who was I to think I was exempt from suffering and rejection? My persuasive personality; my well prayed, considered, and elder-approved decisions; my logical argumentation; my eagerness to engage with every objection; and my idealistic good intentions were not going to rescue me. They were idols I thought would bring security, but they ultimately threatened to take the place of God in my life.

By God's grace, I realized that a large part of my exhaustion came not from the opposition I faced but from my own attempts to placate the opposition. This was consuming all my time. After I had gone home from work, I was still at work in my mind, replaying conversations of the day, planning how to get in front of the right people, plotting what arguments would convince them to respect my position and acknowledge that what we were doing was from the Lord. It was debilitating to constantly gather evidence that would prove my innocence in every conversation, in the hopes of winning the public relations battle. Who wants to do that? It was a spiritual dead end to continue praying and begging God to do something that he never promised to do, something that he explicitly did not do for David, Moses, or even Jesus in this earthly life, which was to have the masses affirm their actions and words. I realized that God promised the opposite: that people would revile us, persecute us, and say all manner of evil falsely against us. We would be blessed in this suffering. It turned out that my insecurity about feeling unqualified to do my job, the wounds from The Committee, and my pride in thinking I deserved something better all conspired to lure me into a kind of pastoral overwork that it is hard to stop merely by accountability groups, scheduling, and setting more reasonable goals.

But in his kindness, God did stop it. He eventually sent The Committee and their co-conspirators away, not coincidentally around the seven-and-a-half-year mark of my tenure. The elders finally exercised church discipline on some of the ringleaders, and the rest left confident that their departure would deal a death blow to the church and my employment there. However, that was not what stopped the overwork. It stopped not in year seven but in year five. It stopped before the rescue came from God and before the opposition went away. It stopped at that table in the library—or at least that was the beginning of the end. It stopped when God, in his kindness, pointed out this deceptively hidden sin in my life and, in his grace, gave me another gift from the Holy Spirit through Psalm 27. I memorized it and clung to it daily—hourly even—until the storm passed. Instead of letting me entertain a bunch of ways to get people to approve of me, the Lord gave me this psalm to remind me that I don't have to be afraid because the Lord is my light and my salvation. The psalm told me that in the day of trouble, God will set me high upon a rock. It reassured me that even if my parents reject me, the Lord will receive me. The psalm promised me that during false accusations and attacks, I will see the goodness of the Lord in the land of the living. The psalm insisted that instead of trying to please people, I should be strong, take heart, and wait for the Lord. Even young people grow tired and weary. They, too, stumble and fall, but those who wait on the Lord will renew their strength. They will run and not grow weary; they will walk and not grow faint. (See Isa 40:30.)

Jim Samra is the senior pastor of Calvary Church in Grand Rapids, Michigan. He holds the PhD in New Testament from Oxford University.

"What You Are Doing Is Not Good": Exodus 18 and Pastoral Overwork

Steven S. Tuell

As I write this, tennis star Naomi Osaka and gymnastics great Simone Biles have both chosen to withdraw from some competitions to conserve their mental and emotional health. Their controversial choices have put self-care into the headlines.[1] By contrast, clergy far too often ignore self-care, with devastating personal results. The damage done by pastoral overwork and burnout has often been addressed—and rightly so.[2] But perhaps less explored are the consequences of pastoral overwork for the churches those pastors serve. I am a Hebrew Bible scholar rather than a parish minister or a "practical" theologian (which I find to be a singularly odd expression because what theology worth its salt is *not* practical?). So my approach to this issue will be exegetical. In Exodus 18, Moses's father-in-law Jethro, after observing Moses through what appears to be a typical workday, tells him, "What you are doing is not good. You will surely wear yourself out, both you and these people with you" (Exod 18:17-18).[3] My investigation will consider this rare critique of Moses in its context, Exodus 18:1-27, and the implications of the remedy Moses pursues following Jethro's advice. Our passage frankly addresses the integrity of people in positions of leadership and the dangers of overwork and burnout. However, it also has implications for the sharing of power in Christian communities and for our need of a trusted friend and mentor.

Exodus 18 is an old northern, or E, tradition.[4] Notice that apart from Exodus 18:1b, 8-11, which use the Divine Name *Yhwh* (typically rendered as "the LORD"),[5] the Divine is referred to throughout this chapter as "God" (Hebrew *'elohim*; cf. Exod 18:1a, 4, 5, 12 [twice], 15, 16, 19 [three times], 21, 23). Northern traditions in Scripture do use *Yhwh* ("the LORD") once the Name is revealed to Moses (Exod 3:9-15), but they remain reluctant to use it too frequently. Further, Moses's father-in-law is called Jethro here (Exod 18:1, 2, 5, 6, 9, 10, 12; cf. Exod 3:1; 4:18) rather than Reuel, the name used in the southern J epic (Exod 2:18; cf. Num 10:29).[6] The focus on Moses in this chapter is also typical of northern traditions. What is surprising, however, is that this passage is *critical* of Moses. Elsewhere, northern traditions exalt Israel's liberator (e.g., Num 12:6-8; Deut 5:1-5). By contrast, this chapter is remarkable for its very *human* portrayal of Moses.[7] The Israelites have come to Horeb, the mountain of God (Exod 18:5),[8] where Moses had received God's call to deliver the Hebrews (Exod 3:1) and where in the following chapters (Exod 19–31) God's Law will be revealed. This takes them into Midianite territory. Jethro, priest of Midian and father-in-law of Moses, comes to the Israelite camp, bringing with him Moses's wife Zipporah and his two sons,[9] Gershom and Eliezer. We are told that Moses had sent them away earlier (18:2-4), perhaps prior to his return to Egypt. At least according to this tradition, Moses seems to have taken steps to protect his family from danger.[10]

At their reunion, Moses tells Jethro of the LORD's deliverance of Israel from Pharaoh and from the hardships they have faced so far in the wilderness. Jethro rejoices and declares "the LORD is greater than all gods" (18:11). Indeed, the Midianite priest offers a sacrifice to the LORD, followed by a sacred meal in which Moses's brother, the priest Aaron, also participates (18:12). This scene would have been highly significant to the old northern priestly families who preserved this tradition. Through much of Israel's history, the right to serve as priests was denied those northern Levites. The southern Jerusalem priests claimed that only they, the rightful descendants of Aaron, could offer sacrifices.[11] But in this northern tradition the right to priestly service is given even to Moses's Midianite father-in-law, with Aaron himself giving his blessing by eating bread with Jethro "in the presence of God" (18:12).[12] A similarly inclusive approach to ministry is found in the parallel to this passage in Numbers 11:11-17.[13] There, Moses has no problem with Eldad and Medad who, despite not having been present at the consecration of the seventy elders, spontaneously prophesy at the spirit's prompting: "Would that all the LORD's people were prophets, and that the LORD would put his spirit on them!" (Num 11:29; cf. Mark 9:38-40). Jethro stays with Moses, watching quietly as his son-in-law works through a long day. Only at the day's end does Jethro question what he has seen: "What is this that you are doing for the people? Why do you sit alone, while all the people stand around you from morning until evening?" (18:14). There is an ambiguity in this question not apparent in translation. The Hebrew *la'am* could mean not "for the people" but "*to* the people (cf. Gen 12:18; 20:9; 26:10)—perhaps already implying that Moses's actions are harming and not helping them.

Moses's answer (18:15-16) reveals a threefold job description. First, the people come "to inquire of God" (18:15). In the Hebrew Bible, to "inquire of [Hebrew *darash*] God/the LORD" often means to consult a prophet concerning God's will (e.g.,1 Kgs 22:8//2 Chr 18:7; 2 Kgs 3:11; 8:8; 22:13, 18//2 Chr 34:21, 26). So Moses is a *prophet*. In fact, we could perhaps more accurately say that Moses is *the* prophet: Deuteronomy 34:10 explains, "Never since has there arisen a prophet in Israel like Moses, whom the LORD knew face to face." This does not mean that Moses was engaged in fortune-telling, predicting the future of each inquirer—what we may think of today when we hear the word "prophet." Rather, Moses is God's messenger, communicating God's will to the people. Second, Moses is a *judge*: "When they have a dispute, they come to me and I decide between one person and another" (18:16). The roles of prophet and judge are not entirely distinct; Deborah was both prophet and judge (Judg 4:4-5), as was Samuel (1 Sam 3:20-21; 7:15-17). However, in Deuteronomy 21:1-5 the task of deciding matters of law is assigned not to prophets but to *priests*. This puts a new spin on the role Moses is seen to fill in this text. The priests were also given a limited, semi-prophetic role: they could use the Urim and Thummim (apparently a sacred lot) to "inquire of the LORD" (Deut 33:8; for how the sacred lot was used, cf. 1 Sam 14:3, 41-42 and 23:1-6). As prophet and judge, Moses, it seems, is filling a priestly role as well.

This impression is strengthened by the third role Moses holds in Exodus 18:15-16. Moses is a *teacher*: "I make known to them the statutes and instructions of God" (18:16). Here again, we might say that Moses is *the* teacher (Deut 4:1-5), as he is the one who will receive the Law from God on Horeb. However, teaching the law was a task particularly assigned, in all the traditions, to the priestly house of Levi (e.g., Lev 10:11; Deut 24:8; Ezek 42:23-24; Mal 2:6-7). So, by describing Moses as prophet, judge, and teacher, Exodus 18:15-16 may also be claiming for Moses another role: priest. From the viewpoint of the old northern priestly families, this would have been important, since many appear to have traced their own descent from Moses himself.[14] For the purposes of this study, this indicates yet another burden placed on Moses, which he evidently believes that he must bear alone (Exod 18:14, 18; cf. Num 11:14). Jethro responded to this inhuman workload as any caring parent would.[15] He told Moses, in no uncertain terms, "What you are doing is not good" (18:17)! First, it is not good for *Moses*, and for obvious reasons: "You will surely wear yourself out. . . . For the task is too heavy for you; you cannot do it alone" (Exod 18:18). Long before contemporary psychotherapists came up with the term "burnout," Jethro described the condition exactly.

But the danger was not to Moses alone, as the Hebrew of Jethro's initial question ("what are you doing *to* the people") has already implied. In full, Jethro says, "You will wear yourself out, both you *and these people with you*." What Moses is doing is not only self-destructive but is destructive to the community as well. The workaholic's conceit is always, "I can't quit now. They're all depending on me." That may be true—but if it is, then "they" are all being deprived of their rightful opportunity to make their own decisions and live their own lives. Jethro's proposal of delegated authority not only gives Moses a much-needed rest but also empowers the community. Like Moses, we may try to "do it all" for the best of reasons, out of a profound desire to help. However, that sort of "help" swiftly becomes coercive, even pathological—not ministry but codependency. Once more, Jethro diagnosed the disease long before it was given its own label in the psychotherapeutic dictionary. Jethro proposes that Moses seek out "able men among the people, men who fear God, are trustworthy, and hate dishonest gain" (Exod 18:21). Apart from its restriction to men, could scarcely be improved on today for identifying people in our communities worthy of the task of leadership. What is more, Jethro confidently expects Moses to discover that such people are not rare. He will find enough to place some "over thousands, hundreds, fifties and tens" (18:21). Another conceit of workaholics is the idea that they are irreplaceable: "I have to do it. No one else can or will." Parker Palmer refers to this misconception as "'functional atheism,' the belief that ultimate responsibility for everything rests with us."[16] Jethro gently informs Moses that God can work through others, too; there are plenty of people capable of sharing his burden.

Notice that Jethro does not tell Moses to stop caring or even to change his job description. Moses is to continue in his priestly role, as prophet, judge, and teacher: "You should represent the people before God, and you should bring their cases before God; teach them the statutes and instructions and make known to them the way they are to go and the things they are to do" (18:19-20). The cure for Moses's burnout—and ours—is certainly not quietism, noninvolvement, or apathy. Rather, Jethro tells Moses to go right on doing what he has been doing but with a difference. Moses must acknowledge that he cannot, and should not, do it all alone—that he needs help. The system Jethro describes provides for a far more efficient means of dealing with questions and conflicts. The first recourse, apparently, would be to the judge appointed to you personally: one for every ten Israelites. Jethro recognized that Moses could not possibly be personally involved in the life of every Israelite. But in this way, every member of the community could talk to someone who knew them well. Similarly, John Wesley divided the first Methodists into classes, or bands—small groups for prayer and support that met weekly: "To speak each of us in order, freely and plainly, the true state of our souls, with the faults we have committed in thought, word, or deed, and the temptations we have felt since our last meeting."[17] Jethro also proposed providing higher courts of appeal: judges over fifties, hundreds, and thousands. These persons could deal with problems too severe or widespread for the judges over tens. Only the most important cases would then be appealed ultimately to Moses himself (Exod 18:22).

Apparently, Jethro's proposal spares Moses a great deal of work. But that is by no means all that it does. Remember Jethro's observation that the people, as well as Moses, were being worn out by the old ways. They had no voice, no real participation in decision-making. But once this program is in operation, "they will bear the burden with you" (18:22). Jethro's proposal shares power and responsibility broadly among the people whose daily lives are affected by the decisions made. Jethro predicts that this program will lead to greater satisfaction and tranquility: "all these people will go to their home in peace" (18:23).

Jethro's solution to Moses's overwork involves, to put it baldly, the creation of an institutional bureaucracy.[18] Yet, because this plan distributes decision-making over all Israel, it results in a system of justice that is *more* personal, not less. The institution Jethro creates is not a replacement for caring but a means of caring more effectively. So too, in the New Testament, practical matters of ministry required organizational solutions, even during Jesus's lifetime. The Twelve served as Jesus's inner circle of followers, and a group of three leaders within the Twelve (Peter, James, and John) were often singled out for special revelations (as on the Mount of Transfiguration: Matt 17:1-8; Mark 9:2-8; Luke 9:28-36) and particular reproof (James and John in Mark 10:35-40 and Matt 20:20-23; Peter in Mark 8:31-33 and Matt 16:21-23). Beyond the Twelve, others who followed Jesus played important organizational roles—including, Luke tells us, women of independent means, such as Mary Magdalene, "who provided for them out of their resources" (Luke 8:3).

In Acts and the letters of Paul, we see practical matters of administration and ministry leading to the creation of church offices: deacons, elders, and bishops. Indeed, Paul affirms that the Spirit has a task for every member in the body of Christ (1 Cor 12:4-11, 27-31). One might compare the offices of the church described in the New Testament with the "officers over thousands, hundreds, fifties, and tens" established by Moses following Jethro's advice.

What lessons applicable to our current circumstances can we draw from Jethro's practical admonition to this son-in-law? Andrew Purves addresses his transformational book *The Crucifixion of Ministry* primarily "to busy, tired, somewhat depressed, midcareer, and fed-up ministers who can't carry the load of ministry any longer"[19]—in short, to pastors like Moses in Exodus 18! At the beginning of his book, Purves describes a conversation with his wife about her frustration with pastoral ministry, "that no matter what she tried, nothing seemed to change."

> Suddenly, I mean out of the blue, I had the insight that there is little, maybe nothing, we who are ministers of the gospel can do that really changes things. If anything worthwhile is to happen, Jesus has to show up. . . . Walking on the beach, I was suddenly aware that our attempt to be effective ministers is a major problem. We are in the way. Our strategies, action plans, pastoral resources and entrepreneurial church revitalization techniques have become not the solution but the problem. Our ministries need to be crucified. They need to be killed off. What if Jesus showed up? That's our only hope. Our people don't need us; they need Jesus. Our job is to bear witness to him.[20]

The purpose of his book, Purves writes, "is to offer a perspective on ministry and illustrate a practice that liberates ministers from the grind of feeling that 'It's all up to me.'"[21] That perspective begins with a crucial insight: "Conceiving ministry as *our* ministry is the root problem of what ails us in ministry today." Instead, "Ministry should be understood as a sharing in the continuing ministry of Jesus Christ."[22] L. Roger Owens describes a different sort of problem with the goal-driven ministry Purves decries: what if it *succeeds*?

> My problem was that I was doing it well and seeing results. I'd put on the mask of the visionary leader and I wore it convincingly. But

> after five years of wearing it, the mask was beginning to chafe. . . . I'd been going against the grain for five years, and was suffering because of it—physically, emotionally, psychologically, spiritually. I was contemplating how to get out.[23]

For Owens as for Purves, the way forward is a reorientation away from "practicing ministry with the unconscious assumption that if I don't make something good happen here it never will"[24] and back toward Christ through contemplative spiritual practice. Part of trusting in God is trusting that God is at work in ways we do not know and cannot see or control.

Another point worthy of note is that we need to find a Jethro of our own. Each of us needs someone who knows us well and loves us enough to confront us with hard truths. In Judaism, this truth finds expression in Mishnah: "Joshua ben Perahiah used to say: appoint for thyself a teacher, and acquire for thyself a companion and judge all men with the scale weighted in his favor."[25] Seek out a spiritual director or covenant group, and see them regularly. We would do Jethro's wise counsel a disservice if we did not mention a theme that runs through the entire plan. Jethro begins with a blessing: "I will give you my counsel, and God be with you" (18:19). The people sought out to be judges, he directs, must be people of reverence who "fear God" (18:21). Finally, Jethro concludes by saying, "If you do this, and God so commands you, then you will be able to endure" (18:23). Jethro's counsel is *godly* counsel. He places it before Moses for prayerful consideration; only if Moses is commanded by God to take this step should the counsel be followed at all.[26]

To be sure, this tells us something important about Jethro. As a wise counselor, he was also a person of faith, willing to submit his own plans to the direction and guidance of God. But Jethro's stipulation that the installation of judges should only take place at God's command also tells us something important about the system itself. Note that Moses followed his father-in-law's advice, as 18:24-26 describes. Although God's command is not explicitly described, we can assume that Moses believed this structure to represent God's will. As Walter Houston observes, "There is no distinction between divine revelation and practical wisdom: the latter is as much the will of God as the former."[27] God is understood, then, to be at work in this institutional structure just as God was at work through Moses himself.

One final note on Jethro as wise counselor: when the job was done, "He went off to his own country" (18:27). Jethro did not have to stick around and compulsively fiddle with the structure he had devised. Nor did he have any need or desire to be a back-seat driver, looking over Moses's shoulder. Jethro was *himself* able to let go, trusting that God was at work and trusting Moses to handle matters that arose as Moses saw fit. In other words, Jethro was that rare and wonderful commodity: an advisor who was able to take his own advice.

Steven Tuell is the James A. Kelso Professor Emeritus of Hebrew and Old Testament at Pittsburgh Theological Seminary in Pittsburgh, Pennsylvania. He holds the PhD in Hebrew Bible from Union Theological Seminary (now Union Presbyterian Seminary)

Winded Prophet

Bryan Dunagan

A few years ago, I took a graduate course on spirituality and ministry at Fuller Theological Seminary, taught by the late Dallas Willard. His opening words on the first day of class were not what I expected. "My prayer for you and my hope for your life," he said, "is that you would never hurry again." I quickly wrote down every word, eager to master the material and move on to his next illumined topic. No time should be wasted; any and all moments with the great Dr. Willard ought to be maximized. He continued, "Hurry is the enemy of the spiritual life. God never gives anyone too much to do. If you have too much to do, then God didn't give it to you." Those words pierced me. As a young pastor, I had grown accustomed to the frenzied pace of pastoral work in the center of the big city. I was unable to see the extent to which lustful achievement in ministry had simply morphed into a more Presbyterian, acceptable, decent-and-in-order form within the church. Later that week, as part of the course, Willard instructed us to spend twenty-four hours in complete silence. Outside of that dynamic, the only other rule was that we do nothing. No productivity, no studying, no advanced reading. He told us we could sit with Scripture as long as it had nothing to do with a sermon or class project. To say that I was stretched would be a more spiritual version of how I really want to describe it. This task was remarkably beyond my comfort zone.

In the first few years of ministry, I found myself bragging to colleagues about how hard I worked and how busy I was. I would attend a conference or interact with friends from other churches and almost proudly wear my busyness as a badge of honor. A mentor once told me that our identity is caught up in what we brag about.

Hustle was becoming an idol. When we mix our achievement-obsessed culture with the expanse of technology now accessible at our fingertips, with the mere touch of a button or a word spoken to Siri or Alexa, the result is a level of unprecedented hyper-hurry. Bestselling author and president of Barna Group, David Kinnaman coined a phrase to describe an accelerated, complex culture marked by "unlimited access, profound alienation and a crisis of authority" as "digital Babylon"[1] in his book, *Faith for Exiles*. We are—everyone, the lot of us—tempted to post, update, Instagram, text, tweet, TikTok, like, comment, friend/unfriend, and share with the world the blizzard we just ordered at Dairy Queen. One heartbreaking result is history's most distracted and inward-facing generation.

A story is told in 1 Kings 19 about the prophet Elijah on the heels of his greatest, boldest achievement as a servant of God. He had more reasons to brag about his achievements and industrious productivity than anyone. In the showdown on Mount Carmel, Elijah took on the idol-worshiping prophets of Baal and the king and queen who were on their side. With unbending courage, Elijah called them out for their hypocrisy and idolatry in front of the entire nation of Israel. He schooled the false prophets, defeating them at their own game. Then, as a kind of victory dance, he called down rain from the skies and ended a severe drought. According to the writer of 1 Kings, "Ahab told Jezebel all that Elijah had done, and how he had killed all the prophets with the sword. Then Jezebel sent a messenger to Elijah, saying, 'So may the gods do to me and more also, if I do not make your life as the life of one of them by this time tomorrow'" (1 Kgs 19:1-2). One would think that after his landslide victory over the queen and her prophets, Elijah would know this is an empty threat. But her words sent him into a complete tailspin: "Elijah was afraid and ran for his life" (19:3). He ran from Jezreel to Beersheba, some hundred miles away (if you read the whole story, Elijah is always running places). "He came to Beersheba . . . and left his servant there. But he himself went a day's journey into the wilderness and came and sat down under a broom tree. And he asked that he might die" (19:3-4).

This leader single-handedly defeated the false prophets. God showed up in a stunning demonstration of power. It was a public victory seen by all. And then he hit a wall. Elijah typifies the human capacity to surge through a season of life, overcoming significant obstacles and confronting circumstances often beyond one's control. You may experience, like the prophet, great victory and breakthroughs along the way. But then, after a major deadline or a breakthrough project at work, you crash. Your body was feeding off "go-get-it-ness" and survival instinct, but that can only last so long. One day you find yourself in burnout.

My wife was in her last year of nursing school, commuting from Dallas to Atlanta to finish her degree. A few weeks before graduation, our twin infants got sick. And then we got sick. Ali was falling behind in her required clinical hours. We were finishing a renovation project on our house. She was dealing with an irritable, anxious husband who was trying to finish a dissertation on spiritual disciplines and found himself hurrying more instead of less. It was a perfect storm. Ali has an uncanny capacity to push through adversity, but after taking her last exam, she came home and collapsed. The adrenaline and caffeine wore off. She lost it.

Elijah crashed, too. Sometime thereafter, "an angel touched him and said to him, 'Arise and eat.' And he looked, and behold, there was at his head a cake baked on hot stones and a jar of water. And he ate and drank and lay down again" (19:5-6). Finally, Elijah rested. Sometimes the most spiritual thing you can do is rest. The idea with rest is that you do nothing, a feat that for many is easier uttered than actualized. You stop working and creating long enough to learn or relearn that you are not defined by what you generate. Rest is God's way of leading us "beside still waters" (Ps 23:2). Rest is how God restores my soul.

A practice closely related to rest is the spiritual discipline of solitude. In solitude, I withdraw from the expectations, pressures, and demands others impose on me (and that I hoist upon myself), which threaten to shift my identity away from being a child of God to being a person whose value is in their work. I deliberately withdraw from people and ministry and the hurried pace of church life to be alone with my heavenly Father. In solitude, I give up the need to impress or provide for other people. I am not defined by what people think of me. Mostly, solitude is about what you don't do. Next we read, "And the angel of the LORD came again a second time and touched him and said, 'Arise and eat, for the journey is too great for you.' And he arose and ate and drank, and went in the strength of that food forty days and forty nights to Horeb, the mount of God. There he came to a cave and lodged in it" (19:7-9). Elijah came to a mountain—the same mountain where God gave Moses the Ten Commandments—to meet with God. "And behold, the word of the LORD came to him, and God said to him, 'What are you doing here, Elijah?'" (19:10). God wasn't asking Elijah this question because God lacked the geofencing or location tracking data. God wanted Elijah to name the reality of how worn down he really was. "Elijah said, 'I have been very jealous for the LORD, the God of hosts" (19:10). Elijah defended himself: "For the people of Israel have forsaken your covenant, thrown down your altars, and killed your prophets with the sword, and I, even I only, am left, and they seek my life, to take it away" (19:11). He had given so much to God in ministry! He and he alone! Here Elijah took a little liberty in exaggerating the negatives. Burnout often leads us to do this. It causes someone to own more of the burden than is actually theirs. The victim hoists the world on their own shoulders—"I am the only one left." Later on, the writer of 1 Kings reveals that there were 7,000 others still seeking to live faithfully for God. Elijah was not in fact alone.

God instructed Elijah to stand on the mountain as a mighty wind tore through. But God was not in the wind. God then sent an earthquake. But God was not in the tremors. God sent fire, but God's presence was not in the flames. "And after the fire the sound of a low whisper. And when Elijah heard it, he wrapped his face in his cloak and went out and stood at the entrance of the cave" (19:12-13). Later in the course with Dallas Willard, he said, "God will not compete for your attention. Generally speaking, he will not raise his voice." Elijah found God in the unhurried, noncompeting voice of a whisper. This is the prize of solitude. It frees us from the white noise of a chronically distracted world. For a people-pleasing, Enneagram 3, achievement-obsessed idolater-in-recovery, solitude is a profoundly helpful spiritual practice. Early on, I attempted to be heroic about it; in typical fashion, I would seek to achieve as much success in solitude as possible. Now it often comes without any fanfare or recognition, as an extended time in my favorite library on a weekday morning. It is a long walk around the college campus nearby. When I face a pressing decision, I take a half day to find a quiet place where I can be undistracted. I reflect and pray, and I allow God to speak to me in a gentle whisper. As Henri Nouwen wrote,

> In solitude we discover in the center of our own self that we are not what we can conquer, but what is given to us. We listen to the voice of him who spoke to us before we could speak a word, who healed us before we could make any gesture to help, who set us free long before we could free others, and who loved us long before we could give love to anyone. It is in this solitude that we discover that being is more important than having, that life is not a possession to be defended, but a gift to be shared.[2]

The outcome of solitude is steady companionship with Jesus and the readiness to engage in ministry once again with an inward poise and sense of joy. In tracing the Gospel accounts of Jesus, Dallas Willard pointed out that the majority of Jesus's disciplined life was practiced in the solitude and quiet that preceded serving the needs of others. Drawing from Paul's use of gymnasium language, Willard likened the life of the disciple to that of an athlete whose preparation comes through consistent training outside the public eye.[3] He drew a helpful distinction between the legalistic concept of trying harder and the wise training that cooperates with the grace of Jesus in a disciple's life. In *The Spirit of the Disciplines*, a classic work of Willard's, he underscores the counterintuitive reality that spiritual practices can ultimately lead to a life marked by the ease and power seen in the life and ministry of Jesus, "flowing from the inner depths, acting with quiet force from the innermost mind and soul of the Christ who has become a real part of us."[4]

I have a pastor friend who talks about the volume, variety, and intensity of people's brokenness and the particular crucible that involves daily walking alongside those in his church. Recently, this friend took a sabbatical. He ditched his cell phone, bought a burner phone, and told his elder board that under no circumstances were they to contact him unless the sanctuary was on fire. The church he served was in the middle of a capital campaign, and in the first week of his sabbatical they learned that the cost of the project was double what they had raised. No call. Every day the pastor drove by the church as he dropped his kids off and picked them up from school. He noticed that there was no construction happening and, perhaps naturally, wondered why. With each day and no progress on the project, he found himself more and more tempted to check in and solve the problem, but he never did. The rest and restorative work that God was doing in his interior life was simply too important. Honestly, I don't think I could have done it.

A few years ago, my wife and I were walking together through a dark night of the soul. For years, we had been trying to start a family. It wasn't working out how we had hoped. In the middle of everything, I remember taking a day off to do nothing and find solitude with Jesus. I went to a Catholic retreat center on the Chattahoochee River in Georgia and did something I did not think was possible through ordinary means of grace—I turned off my phone. Yup, powered it all the way down. What I saw that day, or was allowed by God to see over the course of those hours spent in solitude, was how comfortable I had grown in hiding behind my busyness. The pace of life and the volume, variety, and intensity of ministry had become for me a carefully constructed avoidance strategy. It allowed me not to have to deal with the pain, the loss of control, and the not knowing that defines infertility. What I remember from that day on the Chattahoochee River was not some knock-me-out-of-my-chair, audible voice from heaven. It was more like a gentle whisper: "Bryan, I'm in this. I am with you. Would you trust me in this?"

After confronting Elijah with his fear, self-preoccupation, and inadequacy, God spoke once more to the prophet: "Go, return on your way to the wilderness of Damascus. And when you arrive, you shall anoint Hazael to be king over Syria. And Jehu the son of Nimshi you shall anoint to be king over Israel, and Elisha the son of Shaphat you shall anoint to be prophet in your place" (1 Kgs 19:15-16). God sent Elijah back "on his way," back to doing the work of a prophet. God summoned him back to what he was always gifted and called to do. Solitude and rest were for a season. With a gentle whisper, God reminded the winded runner of his truest identity and then invited Elijah to join God once again in the renewal of the people. God does the same for us.

Bryan Dunagan (1979–2023) was the senior pastor of Highland Park Presbyterian Church in Dallas, Texas. He held a Doctor of Ministry (DMin) degree from Fuller Theological Seminary.

How "Inefficiency" with God Prevents Pastoral Burnout

Micah Lang

Early in my ministry, I felt a deep conviction that I wanted to be a marathon pastor. I wanted to be one of those rare pastors who didn't sacrifice his physical health, emotional health, or family health on the altar of ministry, only to burn out in five to ten years. The temptation to go at a burnout pace is strong in ministry. The needs are so great. Our time is so limited. Our passion is so strong. Greg Gilbert notes that our relationship to work will always lean toward *idleness* or *idolatry*, and both are "deadly misunderstandings of how God wants us to think about our [work]."[1] All pastors face the incredible demands and desires of ministry, and many are crushed under the weight. I love meeting with other pastors and asking how they are doing. More often than not, they share how busy and stressed they are. I sometimes ask, "Could you keep up this pace for the next forty years?" Their response is strikingly consistent. They often laugh and say, "Oh, absolutely not!" My next question is simple: "Then why are you doing all this?"

I want to serve God in ministry, should God allow it, for the rest of my life and then, as an older pastor friend says, "die while still in the game." The commands for gospel workers to *endure* are numerous in Scripture. If you, like me, desire to endure, you must see that it will not happen if you are okay with unhealthy rhythms. If you never have times of Sabbath rest, times of spiritual renewal, times of solitude and silence, you will burn out. It is inevitable. Something or someone will break down. As Christopher Ash rightly said, "Burnout is a terrible price to pay for Christian zeal."[2] My goal in writing this is to do two things for weary pastors. First, I aim to ground you with biblical truths that stay the lies of ministry idolatry. Second, I aim to exhort you to implement a practice that nurtures balance and endurance for the long haul.

I remember the day I was approached by a man I had been witnessing to. He was kicked out of his apartment and plunged instantly into homelessness. I grabbed him some lunch, prayed with him, and then drove around with him for two hours to all the shelters. Every single one was full. Our town has a lot of impoverished and homeless people. I knew I had to get home and keep a commitment to my family, so I gave him cash, dropped him off at a place where I knew he would be safe, and then drove home. I will never forget the desperate look on his face as I drove off. I was unable to meet his needs at that moment, and the weight of it was crushing. I arrived home and cried in the driveway. I prayed, "God, you have to help me. I need to give this over to you so that I can go inside and serve my family." I had done all I could, and I needed to surrender the rest.

I believe it was Peter Scazzero who said pastors try to be God in three ways: (1) Pastors want to be all-knowing (having the answer to every question). (2) Pastors want to be all-powerful (able to fix every problem). (3) Pastors want to be ever-present (available for every situation). Perhaps you connect with one or more of these desires. But the problem is that we are not God. We can never be all-knowing, all-powerful, or ever-present. We are not God and have to be okay with that. Paul felt this when God sent him a thorn in the flesh to keep him from "becoming conceited" (2 Cor 12:7). God intentionally limited Paul and humbled him so that he would not think too highly of himself. And amid Paul's desperate prayer and pleading, God came to him: "My grace is sufficient for you, for my power is made perfect in weakness" (2 Cor 12:9). God is so jealous for glory that he will not allow your ministry for God to become your god. The weight of the needs around us will crush us unless we become content with not being God. We will never prioritize setting aside special times of pursuing God if we think we must be and do what only God can be and do.

Grounding Truths

If we are to face the immense needs and burdens of ministry without being crushed by them, we need to see ourselves in light of the power and glory of God. Thankfully, God is not stingy in comforting weary laborers. Ground your heart in these truths when you feel limited, inadequate, or weak.

God does not need us.

This truth is often affirmed and seldom lived out. God is completely self-sufficient and is orchestrating God's purposes in the universe just fine without us. Psalm 50:12 says, "If I were hungry, I would not tell you, for the world and its fullness are mine." Pastor, God does not need you. God invites you into this work out of the loving goodness of God's heart. Stop trying to be Jesus. You do not have the answer to every question (omniscient), solution to every problem (omnipotent), or time for every person (omnipresent). Rest in this. God's church will be just fine without you. You are not her savior.

God knows our limitations.

I take great comfort in knowing that God is not ignorant of who is on God's team. Psalm 103:14 says, "He knows our frame; he remembers that we are dust." Maybe you feel like no one understands the pressures and time limitations and personal weaknesses you have. But God does. God knows you are a limited, weak human being. God is not a taskmaster rejoicing to watch you sweat and toil but a father who knows you deeply and has compassion for your weakness.

God uses us in our limitations.

As a bi-vocational pastor, I am often reminded of how God gets the glory for any fruit that comes from my ministry. Often, I wish I had more time, better answers, better solutions, or simply didn't need to take breaks. But often, in those moments when I give the little I have, God brings divine power to bear, and (as 2 Corinthians 12 says) it is "perfected in my weakness." God knows you didn't have as much time for sermon prep this week, that you needed to cancel a meeting because your child was sick, or that your counsel was not remotely impressive. But this is so that God's strength can be displayed and so God can get the glory. God uses you even when you have little to give. Weary pastor, feeling the weight of all you wish to do and be, know in the depths of your soul that your weakness and limitations are part of God's plan. You don't need to despise them. You need to boast in them so that "the power of Christ may rest upon you" (2 Cor 12:9). God gives sleep to those he loves (Ps 127:2). God doesn't want your sacrifices; God wants your heart (Ps 51:16-17). Rest in this. God doesn't need you. God knows your limitations. And God uses you in your limitations.

Having "Inefficient" Time with God

Why do you need to be "inefficient" in your time with God? Let me explain. I am a bi-vocational pastor. I also am a very "efficient" person. I work hard and smart. I try to accomplish the most I can with my limited time. Unfortunately, this can creep into my relationship with God. I try to get in as much Scripture, prayer requests, or spiritual disciplines as I can with the limited time I have. The problem is that though this is good for a vocation, it is terrible for a relationship. Imagine if your spouse felt that every time they were with you, you had to work through an agenda? This is not how we should be with God. Makoto Fujimura observed that the Industrial Revolution changed the thinking of our world to view everything in terms of its *usefulness*. We see something as valuable only if it is *efficient* in being useful to us. However, this is not the value system of God towards us. God is completely self-sufficient. God needs nothing of us or of creation. It follows then that God's desire for us is not based on how "useful" we are to God. God simply loves us and wants to be enjoyed by us. Any usefulness we have to God is only in terms of God's generous grace in bringing us into God's plan out of love. As Fujimura pointedly explains, "We see our existence and value only in terms of 'fixing the world.' The gospel of a Creator who acts out of love, not necessity, liberates us from this bondage."[3]

Lasting a lifetime in ministry requires getting over the desire to be "efficient" in our time with God. We need regular moments of unhindered, undistracted, unrushed time with God. Guard those times. Sacrifice for those times. Enjoy those times. You don't spend time with someone you love because it is "useful" to you. You do so because you love the person and simply enjoy being close to them. If your time with God feels rushed or distracted, you will regret it. We need to live out what we say we believe—that our relationship with God is most important. Do we actually believe it when God says, "Do not let the wise boast in their wisdom; do not let the mighty boast in their might; do not let the wealthy boast in their wealth; but let those who boast boast in this, that they understand and know me . . ." (Jer 9:23-24, NRSVue)?

Pastoral ministry comes with some of the greatest joys and deepest sorrows. I remember a particularly draining season filled with all kinds of pastoral discouragements. I was doubting my effectiveness at discipling others and feeling the weight of bi-vocational ministry. My soul felt sluggish. I was emotionally and physically empty. As it so happened, my daily quiet times were more consistent than they ever had been, but it didn't matter. I still felt empty, tired, and drained. I remember putting the kids to bed one night, coming down the stairs, breaking down on the couch, and weeping in front of my wife. "I just feel like I need a date with Jesus," I said. In my heart, I felt the same way I do when my wife and I are unable to go on a proper date for a while. The daily connection is good, but I craved something special. I wanted unstructured, unhindered, unencumbered time to pursue Christ. My wife said, "Okay. Take tomorrow morning and go spend some time with Jesus!" My wife is pretty awesome. Thankfully, in this instance I followed her advice.

I woke up the next day and went to be with Jesus. I grabbed my Bible, my journal, and a water bottle and drove down the road to the edge of a lake near where I live in southern Maine. I parked myself at a picnic table and spent three hours praying, reading, listening, and journaling. I didn't know what to expect and had no idea if it would make me feel better or not. But it was amazing. I didn't look at my phone. I didn't look at the time. I just gave God my full attention.

And I felt healed. I felt renewed and ready to keep going. Ever since that day, I have prioritized these "mini retreats." I take half a day at least once a month to have unstructured, unhindered, intentional time with God. Now I cannot imagine going without these times in my life. I would put forward this simple practice as something to prioritize in your life and ministry. Jesus did "mini retreats," and so should we.

If there's one human being that we would *not* expect to need those times, it is Jesus. After all, he was God. But that's exactly what we see happen. Jesus prioritized having times of silence and solitude in active pursuit of his Father. He was "led by the Spirit into the wilderness" (Matt 4:1), "went out to a desolate place often" (Mark 1:35; Luke 4:42), and "went up on the mountain by himself to pray . . . alone" (Matt 14:23). Before his ultimate sacrifice, he spent time alone in a garden to pray and seek God (Matt 26:36; Mark 14:32). The reason I'm calling these mini retreats and not daily quiet times is because the Gospel writers seem to express a uniqueness about these times. Jesus would occasionally get away for extended periods for focused prayer and fellowship with God. Jesus prioritized his relationship with his Father. In that relational priority, he set aside times to spend a few hours (or a whole night) in solitude with God. This is not a sabbatical or an annual retreat. This isn't the same as a daily quiet time. This is more like when you go on a date with your spouse. It's a more extended period (often planned ahead) when you spend intentional, unhindered time pursuing the one you love.

Why mini retreats and not something else? Most pastors have categories for a daily quiet time and some kind of extended retreat. I believe these are important, and the mini retreat is not meant to replace them. However, consider marriage again. Imagine a marriage in which the spouses see each other every day but never go on dates together. They have an annual anniversary trip that they enjoy but never have special times of relational pursuit outside of daily rhythms. Would we consider this ideal or healthy? Probably not. I think we should say the same of our relationship with God. The daily rhythms are important, and the long retreats are important. But the mini retreats accomplish something these two do not. I have found several unique ways these mini retreats provide spiritual benefits:

- They offer a regular space to search our souls and look for blind spots.
- They create a regular context to focus on hearing from God in the Bible and responding to God in unhindered prayer.
- They help recenter our affections and renew our joy in God.
- They assist in the fight against feeling monotony in daily quiet times.
- They help establish the priority God needs to have in our lives.
- They steady us when life and ministry feel chaotic.
- They help fuel us for a fruitful return to people.

In many ways, taking a mini retreat is like fasting. We are made to be in fellowship with others just as we are made to eat and drink to sustain life. But when we get away and spend extended time alone with God, it centers us and reminds us of what is most important. We can assess ourselves, enjoy God's presence, and get energized to return to the work God has given us. Here is what I hope is wise counsel regarding these mini retreats.

Get it on the calendar (and guard it).

We schedule the things that are priorities for us. Find a time every month (or more often) when you set aside time to be alone for three or four hours. Guard that time. Don't schedule something else then because you know it is open. It's not open. You have a commitment. You have a date planned. And it's important. Emergencies may happen, but think of it this way. Some emergencies would necessitate canceling a date with your spouse. But it would have to be pretty urgent and important. Use the same criteria for your mini retreats with God.

Plan what you will do (but not everything).

In the same way you may have to call in a reservation or pick out an outfit for a date with your wife, be prepared for your mini retreat. Plan to spend some time meditating on a passage of Scripture, praying for particular things, or reading a book that will grow your affections for Christ. But also plan to have unstructured time with God. Set aside time to be silent and listen or to allow God's Spirit to move you to pray for things you didn't plan for.

Put away technology and other distractions.

This is time for God. Social media and emails can wait a few hours. I try to keep myself from even looking at the time. It won't feel like a retreat if you feel distracted or hurried. Create a space and time where you feel free to be with God without the stresses of life pressing on you. Learn to be okay with silence and solitude.

Be patient and persistent.

New rhythms will feel uncomfortable. You may feel anxious or fidgety the first couple of times. You may have high expectations that seem to go unmet. We cannot force God to give us a visceral experience of God's presence. But we can place ourselves in God's path and patiently wait. Be patient and persistent. This time *will* bear fruit. *Keep your focus on enjoying Christ.* As soon as a mini retreat feels like a box to check, it will become a burden and not a blessing. Remind yourself that you are doing this not to grow in intellect or feel good about yourself but to grow in love for Christ. A time like this will serve to make us more like Jesus but only as our focus is fixed on Christ himself, not our own Christlikeness. We need to want Christ. We don't retreat to be with him so that he will make us better pastors. We retreat to be with him because we must have him. We crave his presence. Our affections are fixed on our savior, and we long to fellowship with him.

Intimacy with Jesus

In the same way that going on a date with your spouse for the first time in a long while may feel awkward, starting a new rhythm of prolonged pursuit of God in solitude may feel awkward. But I implore you to consider adding it to your normal rhythms. Incorporating a pattern of mini retreats into my life has led to an explosion of spiritual and emotional health. These "resets" of my priorities and affections have helped me endure and enjoy the labors of pastoral ministry. You may not think you need this, but as David Matthis rightly puts it, "You may not know how badly you needed silence and solitude until you get to know them."[4]

As Makoto Fujimura expresses, "What do we remember and speak of on our deathbeds? We do not boast of our résumés, or how much money we have in our bank accounts, or our educational degrees or fame. Most likely, we speak of the intangible experience of life, of the most precious treasure that we hold dear, of those we love most."[5] To make it more pointed for pastors, I would state that on our deathbeds we will not boast of our seminary degrees, or how big our church was, or how many conferences we taught at, or how many meetings we had. We will be thinking of how we loved Jesus and how we loved those he entrusted to us. Let the one who boasts boast in this: that he knows and understands the Lord.

On the day of my first mini retreat, I was weighed down and burdened by my own inadequacy. I was pouring myself out for the people in my congregation and didn't see the fruit I was longing for. I had to lament my own fallenness and the unmet desires of my soul for my people. But in that moment when I stopped to listen, I realized that I had let my intimacy with Jesus take a backseat to my ministry for Jesus. In that moment of weakness and surrender I prayed, "God, I don't care how many come on a Sunday. I don't care if people respect me. I don't care if anyone wants to hear what I have to say. God, if I pour out my life for others and, at the end of my life, have nothing to show for it but I can say that I knew and loved you . . . it will be enough for me." At that moment, I felt free. The Lord heard my cry and delivered me from my fears. If I hadn't stopped to look, listen, and be with God, I would have continued plowing along, making the bread of anxious toil when the lover of my soul wanted to give me rest.

When you reach the end of your days and look back, what will you see? Will you realize that you spent all your time and energy trying to be Jesus to others and (in the process) lost your first love? We need a new generation of pastors who love being "inefficient" in their time with God, who get away to be with God for hours without boredom, who regularly drink from the fountain of living water and find nourishment for their souls. Be the pastor who endures forty years with joy because you are so in love with Jesus. God doesn't need you. God knows your limitations and uses you despite them. God wants your heart. Your family and your church need a leader who shows them what it's like to put Christ first. The gospel is for you too. Take your burdens to Jesus, and let his gentle and lowly heart provide rest for your soul. And do it often. I promise you will not regret it.

Micah Lang is the Elder for Preaching and Vision at Redemption Hill Community in Lewiston, Maine.

Clergy Burnout, the Spirit's Fire, and Preaching

Michael Pasquarello III

> Almighty God, on this day you opened the way of eternal life to every race and nation by the promised gift of your Holy Spirit: Shed abroad this gift throughout the world by the preaching of the Gospel, that it may reach to the ends of the earth, through Jesus Christ our Lord, who lives and reigns with you, in the unity of the Holy Spirit, forever and ever. Amen. (Collect for the Day of Pentecost, *The Book of Common Prayer*)

The church was born preaching the gospel and exists to proclaim the gospel—to God and the world. Indeed, the church lives by preaching. Moreover, the vocation of preaching is the Spirit's gift to the church for which the life and speech of its preachers are made faithful and fitting to bear evangelical witness to the incarnate, crucified, and risen Lord of all that is. In the call to preach, we are drawn into the joy of proclaiming the creative and redemptive love of God in Christ, poured out by the Spirit in a foolish abundance that exceeds and transfigures everything and everyone. Proclaiming the "gospel of God's glory" requires the language of praise, which springs from our worship of the Triune God. The language of preaching is thus fashioned by the truth of Christ and inspired, energized, and ordered by the Spirit's love. Liturgical theologian Jean Corbon writes of God as the source or wellspring of Christian preaching:

> The Church of Jesus Christ is the concrete place in history where the Trinitarian mystery is explicitly proclaimed and accepted. Where the Father's offer of self-communication of his only Son and his Holy Spirit finds a free response of praise and thanksgiving. This mystery is represented and shared in a festive way in the liturgy of the Church; it is continually offered and accepted in all the dimensions of the daily life of faith.[1]

As people called to build up the church as the Body of Christ in the world, we do not determine how we conduct ourselves without reference to the church's homiletical memory, recalling in the present God speaking the word in the Spirit's power as the source of all Christian preaching. For example, many who doubt the efficacy or usefulness of preaching in our time may have little acquaintance with or interest in a tradition generated by God's initiative and empowerment that begins with the speaking of creation into being; is amplified through the calling of Israel and the faith generated by its Scriptures; finds its central focus in the history of the Incarnate Word and the creation of the church; has been sustained by the Spirit through the centuries up to the present; and will continue until the consummation of all things in the reign of God. What may come as a surprise to many preachers is that we are able to speak *of* God because we have first been spoken to *by* God.

Rowan Williams, former Archbishop of Canterbury, has written of the "charismatic memory" of the church. By this he means the historical memory activated by the Holy Spirit in the Body of Christ as a form of grace. Williams sees this memory at work in worshiping communities where the Bible, as the primary record of God's self-communication, is read not as a relic of the past but as bearing the present communication of God with us in Christ right now. He notes that the habits of charismatic recall and inherited speech tell us how and why the two certainties that characterize much modern thinking, either the certainty of the present or the certainty of the past, are false for a people called to worship God and serve God's mission through history and time, which have been sanctified by God's incarnate presence.[2] As God's people, then, we live out of the past and live into the future. We walk between memory and hope.

Here Williams's comments on the gift of Christian speech are especially insightful.

> We speak because we are called, invited and authorized to speak, we speak what we have been given, out of our new 'belonging', and this is a 'dependent' kind of utterance, a responsive speech. . . . The integrity of theological utterance [including preaching] . . . does not fall into line with an authoritative communication, but in the reality of its rootedness, its belonging in the new world constituted in the revelatory event or process. . . . God 'speaks' in the response as in the primary utterance: there is a dimension of 'givenness', generative power, and the discovered new world in the work of the imagination opening itself.[3]

I invite readers to hear afresh the narrative of Pentecost in the book of Acts. This originating event of the church's life is generated by the power of the Holy Spirit who is poured out by the crucified and risen Jesus on all flesh, just as he had promised. What I find worthy of our attention as preachers is that Luke tells the story in a manner that recalls how, in Genesis 2:7, God breathed the Spirit into dust and created a human being. In Acts 2, moreover, the Spirit breathes life into Peter, leader of the apostles, who had "crashed and burned" in denying and betraying the Lord who called him to share in proclaiming and demonstrating the arrival of God's kingdom. As far as Peter was concerned, his whole world had come crashing down with the death of Jesus—to which he had contributed. Yes, Peter had worked hard. Peter had been passionate for the kingdom proclaimed by Jesus. Peter had given all he had to the ministry of Jesus. And he was certain he understood exactly what needed to be done to call people into God's reign of justice, mercy, and peace. Still, despite his passionate hard work, Peter had fallen short and failed the Lord when it mattered most. While the New Testament does not use our language of "burnout," I think it is fair to say that when the day of Pentecost arrived, Peter was convinced his time with Jesus had come to a bitter end. The future, which had looked so bright when he first dropped his fishing nets and responded to the summons of Jesus—"Follow me!"—appeared dark and closed. In calling attention to the story of Peter and Pentecost, my aim is to encourage preachers and the congregations they serve, who in a time of church decline and self-preservation may indeed struggle to faithfully worship God. My hope is that a preacher's desire for the Spirit's life-giving power will be rekindled by Peter's witness to Christ, the risen Lord who continues to call us to "follow after" his way of prayerful humility, obedient love, and joyful service that honors God through the gospel proclamation.

I suspect many preachers and congregations feel unnoticed or even dismissed by a church culture that glories in the impressive, trendy, and fashionable. They need inspiration to remain faithful, to go on as living witnesses to a not yet completed glory taking form in the world. And they need hope that despite the constant struggle to remain true, as communities of worship and service, they are positioned to hear afresh the remarkable good news of the Triune God's saving work of reconciliation for all nations and people. They may be assured by God's word that God's work continues "today" in the church's missionary proclamation of the gospel that, in its appeal to be reconciled to God, mediates and actualizes the benefits of God's finished work to women and men.[4] I am keenly aware that many preachers are exhausted and discouraged, "burnt out" from trying to conform themselves and their ministries to the prospects of a culture that values celebrity, entertainment, superficiality, and whatever is propositioned as immediately "useful." Many of them feel they must justify themselves according to standards of ministry that cultivate both pride of success and fear of failure rather than faith that works through sacrificial love poured out by the Holy Spirit in abundance. I have in mind pastors who have been discouraged by the ugliness of "ministry as competition," worn out by presumably "effective" plans and programs that disfigure the beauty of the gospel and diminish desire for the Word. Then there is the additional weight of serving in a cultural environment marked by polarization, cynicism, acrimony, conflict, and contempt. We are a mess and in a mess without yielding to the Holy Spirit's forever transforming, incomparable presence.

The story of Pentecost is a summons to "see" anew the heart of the church's Spirit-inspired vocation: hearing and proclaiming the message of Christ to the world in all we think, say, and do. My hope is that consistently recalling the story of the church's birth will be a welcomed breath of fresh air, inspiring delight in and restoring desire to proclaim the glory of God.[5] Significantly, Pentecost was a time of worship, of giving glory to God, in the life of God's people. It was a liturgical event, the "work of the people," that paradoxically was a day of rest and renewal for offering themselves in thankful praise to God for faithfulness and abundant goodness. At the heart of Pentecost is the joyful acknowledgment of God's generous provision in the ordinary cycles of planting, tending, waiting, and harvesting. Moreover, Pentecost marks the remembrance of the events at Sinai, of God's giving of the Law to Israel accompanied by signs of fire and thunder. Peter's announcement of Christ as the risen Lord is situated within the story of a pilgrim people gathered to remember the future while considering God's past faithfulness.

A paradigmatic demonstration of apostolic preaching encourages us to see the practice of preaching—its truthfulness, wisdom, character, and manner of speaking—in terms of the church's primary vocation of knowing and praising God in the whole of life as our truest end and joy. Following the example of Peter, what if we were to understand our identity and work as preachers according to the originating story of Israel, Christ, and the creation of the church at Pentecost? What if we were to see ourselves as a pilgrim people rather than mere communicators, consumers, or partisan advocates for particular causes, groups, and agendas; as those persuaded and empowered by the Spirit to boldly confess our incompleteness in returning to worship God, loving one another, and serving the world? What if our preaching begins with confessing that Christian people walk by faith and not by sight, acknowledging that all we are, have, do, and say is the superabundantly generous gift of the Word spoken in the incarnate, crucified, and risen Lord through the Spirit? Here, Lesslie Newbigin's theological assessment of the church's being and action is apt:

> They are the radiance of a supernatural reality. That reality is, first of all, the reality of God, the superabundant richness of the

being of the Triune God, in whom love is forever given and forever enjoyed in an ever new exchange. . . . It is said of this superabundant glory that it has been given to believers in order that they may be recognizable as a community where the love of God is actually tested and known. . . . This is what makes the church a place of joy, of praise, of surprises, and of laughter, a place where there is a foretaste of the endless surprises of heaven.[6]

It worth noting that Peter's sermon in Acts 2 is not simply a lecture, a talk, a life lesson, a topic, an idea, a principle, or a set of rules that "work" when applied by listeners to make their lives better, to "make a difference," or to have a greater impact in the "real world." Nor does Peter speak of Jesus as a heroic and inspiring teacher who was all about "values" such as love, mercy, compassion, and justice. According to Luke's account, Peter's preaching is not dependent on his personality, technique, skill, or capacity to attract, entertain, and excite a crowd. Instead, Peter's bold, daring preaching displays robust confidence in the astonishingly uncontrollable eruption of the "real world"—the radiant light of a new creation shining forth from the Spirit's witness to the presence of the crucified and risen Lord through preaching that extends the story and promise of Israel's God to the nations.

Christian preaching heralds the glorious "end" of all things in the name of Jesus, a message of good news that flows from the depths of a common life of praise generated by God. Spoken as itself an act of worship, such preaching may still serve to "entice and enchant us not only to desire but also to fall in love with God the Trinity, and thereby love our neighbors."[7] Theologian Mark McIntosh notes that, because the church is a life of grace, of divine rather than human initiative, it may itself be a "divine speaking" or "word of God" within the world, a sign of the possibility of a new creation appearing in the midst of the old creation, a provisional yet visible sharing in the life to come that is already a participation in the eternal joy and delight of the Trinity.[8] Luke thus testifies to the beauty of the church raised up by the Spirit in and for the preaching of its good news to the world.

> All who believed were together and had all things in common; they would sell their possessions and goods and distribute the proceeds to all, as any had need. Day by day, as they spent much time together in the Temple, they broke bread at home and ate their food with glad and generous hearts, praising God and having the goodwill of the people. (Acts 2:44-47a, NRSVue)

Perhaps nothing in this story is more offensive and delightful to our modern, technologically savvy, cause-and-effect, "do-it-yourself" approaches to ministry than the notion that God's gratuitous love does not depend on us. The gospel announces that from beginning to end, our lives are not of our own making, management, or control. I suspect Peter, impulsive, brash, self-confident, and assertive disciple that he was, also found this truth rather scandalous, as the Gospels clearly show us. Yet, like Peter, it is in learning to confess that we are sinful creatures of a gracious God that we delight in seeing just how much our lives and words are constituted as gifts rather than possessions, whose purpose is to praise the wisdom and goodness of our Creator.

In Christian worship, as the day of Pentecost reveals, we acknowledge our grateful dependence according to the wisdom displayed in the self-giving of our crucified and risen Lord, through which the Spirit evokes thankful receptivity and energizes glad responsiveness to God who continues to speak creation and salvation into being. There is nothing more urgent in our time than believing and proclaiming the "foolishness" of the cross—the power and wisdom of the gospel that creates both the preacher and people to be a sacrifice of praise and joyful obedience through whom the Spirit bears witness to the renewal of our humanity before God. Rather than the "burnout" that comes from our determined efforts to be competitive, autonomous, and profitable, the fire of the Spirit kindles our hearts with burning desire for the living God whom to know, love, and enjoy is life itself. As Pope Francis states this matter clearly in his apostolic exhortation, *The Joy of the Gospel*,

> A renewal of preaching can offer believers, as well as the lukewarm and the nonpracticing, new joy in the faith and fruitfulness in the

work of evangelization. The heart of its message will always be the same: the God who revealed his immense love in the crucified and risen Christ. God constantly renews his faithful ones, whatever their age: 'They shall mount up with wings like eagles, they shall run and not be weary; they shall walk and not be faint' (Isa. 40:31).[9]

Michael Pasquarello III retired in 2024 as the Methodist chair of divinity; director of the Robert Smith, Jr. Preaching Institute; and director of the Doctor of Ministry program at Beeson Divinity School in Birmingham, Alabama. He holds the PhD in Religious Studies from the University of North Carolina at Chapel Hill

Comfort-curated Ministry

Dave Dack

There is a remote-controlled helicopter in my office that the church doesn't know about (well, they know about it *now*). But more about that in a minute. One of my favorite classes in seminary was Pastoral Arts with Dr. M. Craig Barnes. His example and instruction shaped much of my approach to ministry and leadership. However, the most memorable experience from that class occurred when I asked Dr. Barnes what a new pastor should do if, upon arriving at their first call, they found themselves with extra time. What should I do, for example, if I somehow finish all the relevant weekly pastoral work (sermon, bulletin, meetings, visits, etc.) and for the life of me can't think of what else to do? I'll never forget the expression on his face as he said with amusement, "Trust me, that's not going to be a problem." Which brings me to the helicopter. During my first year of parish ministry, I often *did* have extra time toward the end of the week, and in the late afternoon I would fly my helicopter in our fellowship hall. And I was good at it. The tables and chairs provided a natural obstacle course, and I could execute precision landings on even the smallest carpet stain. Of course, I only flew the chopper after I finished my sermon, prepped the bulletin, planned well for meetings, and called or visited parishioners. But these tasks don't take long at a small church, and I often found myself with an excess of the rarest and most precious pastoral resource: *time*.

This might lead one to believe, as I mistakenly did, that I am not a workaholic. Workaholics don't fly toy helicopters around their church. Even now, after twelve years, whether or not I dive into helicopter piloting practice on any given day, I don't think I've ever worked more than fifty-five hours in a week, and I rarely exceed forty. Clearly, I thought, pastoral overwork is not my addiction, and ministry is not my idol. But addiction and idolatry take many forms. In C. S. Lewis's beloved book *The Screwtape Letters*, Screwtape explains to his nephew Wormwood the difference between gluttony of excess and gluttony of delicacy:

> Our patient's mother . . . is a good example. She would be astonished—one day, I hope, will be—to learn that her whole life is enslaved to this kind of sensuality, which is quite concealed from her by the fact that the quantities involved are small. Because what she wants is smaller and less costly than what has been set before her, she never recognizes as gluttony her determination to get what she wants, however troublesome it may be to others.[1]

Her determination to get what she wants. Now *there's* an addiction I can relate to. I am the patient's mother from Screwtape's letter. My problem is not the *quantity* of ministry but the *quality*. I am determined to get what I want.

This would surprise my church members. When you imagine a pastor determined to get what they want, you may picture a kind of religious tyrant, someone calling all the shots and losing their temper when the bulletin font is the wrong size. I am certainly not that! I can be found on the other extreme of the example, for I am far too agreeable. I end most of my sentences with some version of "only if you really don't mind" or "please feel free to say no." One church member ranked me as the third most approachable person she knew (after Jesus and Santa). I am the quintessential people-pleaser, eager to keep the peace at all costs. *That* is what I want, and I am determined to get it. The way I get it is by avoiding aspects of ministry that make me (and others) uncomfortable. I am a pursuer of "comfort-curated" ministry. There, I said it. I suppose it is kind of natural; everyone avoids discomfort in some way, and I hope the reader can sympathize. I know there is grace. But ministry curated to my comfort tends to become *my* ministry rather than *Christ's* ministry, and in case it doesn't go without saying, that's a bad thing. In fact, it is a really,

really bad thing. As Andrew Purves reminds us in *The Crucifixion of Ministry*, "Too often our ministries are in the way . . . they are not redemptive. Only the ministry of Jesus is redemptive."[2]

Here's how comfort-curated ministry often looks in my context. Since I am a solo pastor, almost everything at the church goes through me at some point. Every event, program, or policy comes to me, even when my approval isn't technically required. This allows me to act as a subconscious but deliberate bottleneck that only lets ministry proceed if I'm comfortable with it. It looks bad when I type it out like that, but there it is. No sense in making it pretty. I'm like a helicopter parent, hovering just close enough to make sure things go according to my preferences. Thus, in my reflexive effort to avoid uncomfortable ministry, I end up with less work than I otherwise might. Or at least, I end up with a more controlled workflow that makes me more comfortable. I say no to things (healthy) but not always for good reasons (unhealthy). This creates the illusion that I do not idolize ministry. I am like Aaron, who took the golden calf and named it Yahweh, hoping that would hide the idolatry of his people-pleasing ministry. In truth, he was just more comfortable with the twenty-four-carat calf than the forty-day smoldering summit. This bottlenecking is highly unfortunate because the best things in our church have happened when I got out of the way. Our weekly after-school program, for example, only happened when I finally put some leaders in a room and said, "You're in charge—go for it!" At first, they bounced all their ideas off me, hoping I would offer approval. After stubbornly refusing to give my input, they finally went on to embracing their newfound permission and then ran with it. They didn't run the program the way I would have, and I thank God for that every day because that's why it's still running.

Comfort-curated ministry is my idol. My addiction is to quality, not quantity. Interestingly, the biblical cover for my particular form of ministry idolatry comes from a popular misunderstanding of Paul's spiritual gifts. In several of his letters, he catalogs many of the gifts with which the Holy Spirit has empowered individuals in the church. First Corinthians 12:4-11 is a perfect example:

> Now there are varieties of gifts, but the same Spirit; and there are varieties of service, but the same Lord; and there are varieties of activities, but it is the same God who empowers them all in everyone. To each is given the manifestation of the Spirit for the common good. For to one is given through the Spirit the utterance of wisdom, and to another the utterance of knowledge according to the same Spirit, to another faith by the same Spirit, to another gifts of healing by the one Spirit, to another the working of miracles, to another prophecy, to another the ability to distinguish between spirits, to another various kinds of tongues, to another the interpretation of tongues. All these are empowered by one and the same Spirit, who apportions to each one individually as he wills. (ESV)

In my experience, our understanding of these spiritual gifts is often less informed by the text itself than by popular psychology. We subconsciously convert "spiritual gifts" into "personality traits" and assume that they are fixed characteristics. We run the biblical text through the cheesecloth of modern psychology and end up distorting both. This allows us to use Scripture as a kind of religious sanction for avoiding things we don't want to do. For example, we can say "That's not my spiritual gift" when we really mean "That makes me uncomfortable, and I don't want to do it." We wrongly assume that discomfort equals un-giftedness and is therefore a legitimate excuse. A fresh, plain reading of Paul's list refutes this distorted caricature of spiritual gifts. Nowhere does he imply that a spiritual gift must align with our comfort zone, and he rather bluntly asserts that the Spirit "apportions to each one individually *as he wills*." Spiritual gifts are not mere personality traits determined by a mixture of nature vs. nurture. They are, by definition, given by the Spirit when and where he wills.

In *A Smile on the Face of God*, author Adrian Plass shares the story of Rev. Philip Ilott, priest of St. Alban's Church on the Isle of Wight. During the 1970s, after attending a local revival meeting, Philip felt called to start a monthly healing ministry at his own church. Unsure of what would happen but convinced of God's faithfulness, he began praying that God would heal the people who came forward during the services. For a while no one was healed. But then Philip was invited to a school for "delicate children" run by a local convent. He was deeply moved by the opportunity to pray for so many disabled children. One little girl in particular stood out to him. When he asked what she would like Jesus to do for her, she was silent. Philip said, "It doesn't matter what the problem is if you've got Jesus living in your heart." The girl replied, "That's it, he can't. He can't come and live in my heart." The girl explained that she had a hole in her heart. Through tears Philip prayed that Jesus would heal the hole in her heart, and a few weeks later that's exactly what happened. She was the first person to receive miraculous healing through Philip's ministry, but she wasn't the last. Miraculous healings would continue for a long time, and many people would experience God's power firsthand. As Plass describes it,

> [Philip's] whole experience of the healing ministry was like that. It was no use posing as a deep and spiritually insightful human being, because it was God who did the healing, God who provided the specialized information, and God who laid down the means and process by which each individual received the help that they needed.[3]

Healing was not one of Philip's personality traits or something for which he was naturally gifted. It was a spiritual gift given by the Spirit as the Spirit willed. Philip's ministry was actually Jesus's ministry all along, which is the way it should be. Truthfully, it is the only way it *can* be. It's easy in pastoral ministry to ignore this powerful and uncomfortable truth. It's easy to catalog our natural gifts and curate "our" ministry accordingly: "Administration isn't my gift." "I'm more of a teacher than an evangelist." "Hospital visits are really more of a deacons' thing." In such ways, we settle like concrete into segmented ministry molds, deftly denying the possibility that the Holy Spirit may gift us for any ministry at any time, if only we would pray and listen and ask. Paul tells us to "eagerly desire the greater gifts," but I wonder if we really do. Comfort-curated ministry is a particularly deceptive form of idolatry and pastoral overwork because it proudly masquerades as the opposite. It looks down on other pastors who work long hours, and it celebrates balance while sacrificing to Baal. I hope I have done my part to expose this devious demon both in myself and in a few readers. Now that we have the revelation, we must seek the remedy.

Some years ago, I had a disturbing dream. I was playing chess with my best friend when our game had reached a critical point. It was my turn to move, but uncertainty paralyzed me. I had a terrifying sense that the outcome of the game depended on my next move and that I would lose if I got it wrong. The thing is, I had no idea what the right move was, so I just sat there brooding in anxiety. My impatient friend urged me to make my move, and I blurted out, "I can't! I don't know which move to make!" Suddenly the whole room became dark, and the mood of the dream shifted into more of a nightmare. My friend leaned over the table with eyes that looked like he'd been possessed, and he said to me in a voice that was not his own: "You need to have more faith!" Then the dream ended. It was a long time before I played chess again. Ever since then, there has been a strange connection between my chess game and my spiritual life. I have noticed that I play better chess when my soul is well, and I play poorly when my soul is restless. Chess has become a kind of checkered canary, signaling shifts in my spiritual health before I would otherwise notice them myself. Because of this admittedly weird correlation, I have also found many of the principles of good chess playing to be helpful analogies for maintaining healthy spiritual practices. They have become a Rule of Life that preserves my soul, which translates into better ministry that worships Christ instead of idolizing comfort.

Before sharing these principles and practices, I have to say I'm not really offering anything new. Spiritual disciplines and Rules of Life are not new concepts, and there are hundreds of excellent examples and authors who have traced paths of faithful ministry for us to follow. Richard Foster, Dallas Willard, and Eugene Peterson are a few of my favorites, and I have recently been encouraged by *A Pastoral Rule for Today* by John P. Burgess, Jerry Andrews, and Joseph D. Small, which surveys the lives and works of historical ministers such as Augustine, Benedict, Calvin, Wesley, and Bonhoeffer, who pioneered Rules of Life that guided generations of Christ-centered ministry.[4] My contribution here seems small by comparison, but it has helped me, and maybe it can help you, too. Eight principles have improved both my chess game and "my" ministry. These principles are not concrete practices; like me, the reader must discover their own applications and rhythms that help them abide by the principles. Still, may you find them a helpful antidote to all forms of idolatrous ministry. They might even improve your chess game, too.

Control the center.

In chess, the center of the board is the most important part of the game. Whoever controls the center controls the outcome. A good chess player will do anything to control the center of the board, and only then do they worry about the rest of the game. Spiritually, Christ is the center of the board, not just for our ministry but for our entire lives. We must develop and guard a Christ-centered life if the rest of our game is to be any good. Christ comes before everything else. Period.

Develop your pieces.

During the opening of a chess game (the first ten to fifteen moves), it is crucial to develop your pieces. This is not the time to fuss over your pawn structure; it is the time to get your bishops and knights out onto the board where they can be useful. Likewise, there is always room for us to develop spiritually. We must never settle for our current position, leaving our best pieces on the back rank while the enemy charges in. We must prioritize spiritual development over fussing about the endless pawn-like tasks of ministry. We must become ever more fluent in prayer, literate in Scripture, and accepting of spiritual direction from our mentors. We must mature in grace and work out our salvation with fear and trembling.

Put your pieces in the place of most potential.

A chess piece is most effective when it is well placed. When your pieces are in the center, they are the most useful. It is from there that their potential can be maximized best. A piece on the side of the board has limited options, but a piece in the center can wreak havoc on the opponent. Are we putting ourselves in the places of most potential? Are we spending time where ministry will be most effective? Do I really need to put in another hour at the office, or is there more potential in visiting the hospital, walking around the city park, or praying through the church directory? Ministry has the most potential when we place ourselves in situations where Christ is already doing his best work.

Connect your rooks.

After developing your pieces and castling your king to one side, it's always a good idea to connect your rooks. Connected rooks occur when both are on the back rank with no other pieces between them. They are defending each other. Disconnected rooks are a liability that can lead to something called a back-rank mate (just Google it), but connected rooks provide a strong foundation for the rest of your game. Spiritually, this is reminiscent of Frederick Buechner's famous vocational advice: "Your vocation in life is where your greatest joy meets the world's greatest need."[5] That is to say, find what brings you joy and connect it to a great need in the world. Ministry to others is always best when it represents genuine overflow from a joyful heart. Joyful ministry is the most selfless kind and the least in danger of becoming an idol.

Find a better move.

You obviously want to make the best move possible in chess. Amateurs and masters alike look for the best move. What separates masters from amateurs, however, is that when masters find the best move, they look for a better one. In ministry, pastors are constantly faced with ambiguous decisions, especially when discerning God's will in a certain situation. When we think we have an answer, we sometimes rush into it without considering that an even better move could be available. Of course, at some point we have to make a move regardless, but it's always worth considering that God might have something in mind that is even better than what we've come up with so far.

See the whole board.

Tunnel vision can destroy your chess game. It's easy to focus on one area of dynamic play on the board only to discover that you forgot about that bishop sitting way back in the corner taking direct aim at your king. Before every move, you must try to see the whole board. Tunnel vision is just as devastating to ministry. We can become so focused on a particular area (Sunday morning worship, small groups, visitation, etc.) that we fail to see the wider kingdom perspective. Jesus said, "Seek first the kingdom of God, and all these things will be added to you as well" (Matt 6:33, ESV). Ministry means zooming out and considering the kingdom, both for our sake and for the sake of the church.

Analyze games.

When I'm playing chess poorly, I lose more games and then quickly start new games in hopes of winning and increasing my rating. But when I'm playing well, I take time to analyze my games, whether I won or lost. Reviewing past play improves future play. Our spiritual lives are no different. It is vital that we analyze the past to discern God's previous and ongoing faithfulness in context. This teaches us to expect God's faithfulness in the future. St. Ignatius's Prayer of Examen is a particularly useful tool for this kind of prayerful analysis.

It's all about the King.

Nothing is more exciting in chess than a queen sacrifice that wins the game. It is the equivalent of a bottom-of-the-ninth, full-count, grand-slam comeback win. Because at the end of the day, the only thing that matters is capturing the king. Even if you must sacrifice every other piece to do it, capturing the king wins the game. Ministry is all about the King. Once everything is said and done, if we and our church members are not resting joyfully in Christ and abiding in him for our dear lives, then something is wrong. All other work—all programs, all worship events, all leadership development, *even ministry itself*—is worth sacrificing if we gain the King in the end. As Paul famously wrote in Philippians 3:8-9, "For his sake I have suffered the loss of all things and count them as rubbish, in order that I may gain Christ and be found in him" (ESV).

Pastoral overwork is not always obvious. The most dangerous idols never are. It takes many forms and tempts all ministers in some way or another, often employing Scripture itself as religious justification, much like the devil in the desert. For God's sake, and for the sake of the church, all pastors must carefully tend to their spiritual lives. We must love the Messiah more than our ministry if our ministry is going to do any good. Do whatever it takes to capture the King. Make *time* for Jesus (which includes making time for relationships with family and friends). It may mean sacrificing some of your ambitions, your projects, your programs, or your reputation as a hard worker. But if you're worried that the sacrifice won't be worth it to gain Christ, trust me, that's not going to be a problem.

David Dack is the Pastor of Lemoore Presbyterian Church in Lemoore, California.

The Work of Rest[1]

Stephen L. Woodworth

Shortly after becoming Pope in the year AD 590, Gregory the Great produced a work titled the *Pastoral Rule* in which he set about the task of describing in great detail the nature, duties, and obligations of clergy in relation to the "heaviness" of their work.[2] Centuries later, in preparation for a "Day of Humiliation" held on December 4, 1655, Richard Baxter published his own work along these lines, *The Reformed Pastor*. Amid rampant complaints against clergy, his treatise was dedicated to "showing the nature of the pastoral work" in an age of growing distrust of ordained ministers.[3] Both Richard and Gregory attempted to speak with authority into what appeared to be widespread confusion about what role pastors ought to play. While far reaching in their influence, neither work was entirely novel in content or aim. In centuries before and after, the issue of pastoral identity was scarcely ever absent from the writings of those concerned about the church.[4] In every epoch since the inception of the Christian movement, pastors, theologians, and scholars of every variety have added their voices to the growing amount of literature dedicated to answering the question, *what is a pastor?* While each author has considered their own era as one of crisis of varying degrees, the sheer multitude of voices throughout time lend themselves to William Willimon's more sobering proposition: "Because of its nature, pastoral identity is never secure. In every age the church must ask, 'What are pastors for?'"[5]

In our own age, the search for pastoral identity is no less persistent. As a new generation gives rise to pastors and theologians, fresh dialogue emerges about the current state of pastoral identity. This is captured well in the sentiments of David Fisher: "The literature on contemporary pastoral ministry is remarkably diverse but tends to agree that we are at a crisis point and that at least part of the problem is pastoral identity in our modern society."[6] The specific reasons given for the current confusion regarding pastoral identity vary greatly. While some suggest this stems from deficiencies in pastoral theology,[7] or the loss of pastoral authority,[8] Eugene Peterson submits that it is due to a great loss of respect for the very term "pastor," which he saw as being "defined by parody and diluted by optimism."[9] While the particular reasons given may wax and wane, the fact remains that it is essential for every pastor to return again and again to the core question of their identity if they hope to remain faithful to their calling. Indeed, as one writer put it, "Doubtless a major cause of 'burnout' in ministry is the blurring of pastoral ministry."[10] While there are numerous causes for this blurring, I want to focus on two issues specifically that can be especially hazardous to pastoral identity in the twenty-first century: congregational expectations and an emphasis on "doing" rather than "being."

Congregational Expectations

To grasp a key cause of pastoral identity issues, one only needs to take a cursory scan of the latest pastor search profiles in the Christian classified section. Churches are looking for someone who is a shepherd, yes, and simultaneously chief executive officer (CEO), fundraiser, expositor, counselor, marketer, spiritual mystic, missionary, and more that goes unspoken or unnamed. In such a climate, pastors often find themselves at the mercy of their congregations' felt needs. Churches appear to be hungry for pastors who are "experts" in every area of faith life. In trying to meet such expectations, many of them find that their pastoral identity is shaped more by external pressures and expectations than internal convictions or values. Reflecting on this dilemma, Brian Williams writes,

> Competing visions, explanations, expectations, and job requirements for pastoral ministry are handed to us from a myriad of sources. Our culture, former pastors, professors, authors, parents, friends, and parishioners all speak into our pastoral identity and,

welcome or not, subtly inform our understanding of what we have been called to, shaping the way we think and act. Becoming clear about the nature of the pastoral call is imperative because we live into those implicit visions we harbor and into explicit visions we esteem and nurture in our mind's eye. Critical to the process of becoming a pastor is to move beyond the stereotyped images of minister we encounter and perpetuate.[11]

Out of all the competing voices Williams alludes to, many pastors will agree that the voice of their congregation tends to speak the loudest. This is not to suggest that a pastor's desire to discern and respond to the real needs of the congregations is wrong. After all, "one cannot serve Christ without serving people."[12] However, the more fundamental problem in most cases is attempting to meet the *misinformed* and *unrealistic* expectations of congregations, whose values are sometimes shaped by business practices or the entertainment industry, not accurate biblical theology. A quick perusal of prominent ministry employment websites reveals that, instead of being led by "pastors," churches are increasingly organizing themselves around leadership teams, boards, and directors. Similarly, instead of looking for "ministers," an increasing number of churches are busy recruiting technicians and producers with a proven track record of creating relevant, inspirational atmospheres. The current atmosphere of church culture lends support to Eugene Peterson's brave and discerning musings:

> Congregations get their ideas of what makes a pastor from the culture, not from the scriptures; they want a winner, they want their needs met; they want to be part of something zesty and glamorous. . . . With hardly an exception they don't want pastors at all—they want managers of their religious company. They want a pastor they can follow so they won't have to bother with following Jesus anymore.[13]

Given these realities, pastors in our current age are experiencing great difficulty developing an internal pastoral identity that is principally separate from the people they serve in the best ways. Identity is a deeply personal matter, as we know, and while community plays a key role in helping people become better aware of themselves, pastors often capitulate in allowing their church to determine their identity for them instead of discovering and illuminating their pastoral identity in a healthier way. As true as this dynamic is, pastors cannot cast all blame on their congregations, for they themselves also contribute to the wreckage by seeking to please people above God. Outward success or failure is not how the Lord assesses ministry, but sometimes the depressingly unpredictable lives pastors and their beloved families face because of their line of work can be a hard lesson to learn. Regrettably, pastors sometimes determine who they are based on what they *do*, not via the internal conviction about who God has called to them first to *be*.

Emphasis on Doing Rather than Being

Right now, the church functions within a world changing at an unprecedented rate,[14] urging many congregations to try to keep up and follow suit. As such, pastors are more and more tempted to embrace new models of ministry with a somewhat suspicious utilitarianism, asking questions like, "Will it work? Is it relevant? Will it produce results?" The risk of being considered archaic or obsolete, it appears, drives pastors and their flocks to the constant pursuit of pragmatic, results-oriented programming. As David Steele comments, "Professional pastoral ministry suffers today from the loss of a sense of accomplishment amidst an ever-increasing burden of busyness and pressure."[15] Richard Neuhaus agreed, and the words he penned over thirty years ago seem as relevant today as ever:

> Pastors harassed by these conflicting expectations and claims upon time and ability are tempted to embark upon an open-ended game of trade-offs. Today I'll be a little of this and a little of that; tomorrow I'll be a little of the other thing and something else. For the conscientious who are determined to keep the game going, it is a certain formula for confusion and collapse.[16]

This overemphasis on "doing" the work of the church is creating an atmosphere of diminished reflection for pastors, which then leads to less clarity about their identity. The danger lies in the often unforeseen consequences that, when a pastor begins to believe the lie that they *are* what they *do*, they can begin to view everything as a task, including the people they serve. This can easily result in what Joe Trull refers to as "clerical agnosia." In his seminal text with James E. Carter, *Ministerial Ethics: Being a Good Minister in a Not-So-Good World*, Trull shared this fitting reflection:

> Every seminarian knows that a call to become a minister of a church is a call to various tasks. Preaching, teaching, counseling, visiting, administrating, promoting, recruiting, leading worship, and doing community service are just a few of their tasks. Today's minister must wear many hats. The unseen danger for the busy religious leader is "clerical agnosia," becoming a minister who mistakes a parishioner for one of his or her hats.[17]

While I noted earlier that congregational expectations play a role in this dilemma for pastors, a more hidden and arguably more powerful source exists within the hearts and minds of some pastors whose insecurities[18] and lack of internal identities cause them to justify their roles daily in constant busyness. Reflecting on his first pastorate, David Fisher writes,

> As I went about my duties—meeting people, tending to the church, preparing for sermons and lessons, and conducting a wider variety of meetings than I had ever imagined—I suddenly was aware that I didn't know *who* I was supposed to be. . . . there is little satisfaction in performance of tasks without a clear and foundational identity. Nothing in seminary prepared me for this identity crisis.[19]

In his typically blunt manner, Eugene Peterson faults the predicament many pastors are afflicted by on a mixture of "vanity" (pastors want to appear important) and "laziness" (pastors allow others to decide how to fill their time).[20] His conclusion is simply, "The adjective *busy* set as a modifier to *pastor* should sound to our ears like *adulterous* to characterize a wife or *embezzling* to describe a banker. It is an outrageous scandal, a blasphemous affront."[21] Burdened by unrealistic congregational expectations and their own attempts to constantly "look busy," pastors in the twenty-first century need robust resources to guide them toward a fresh perspective. However, I do not believe a solution is to be found if pastors simply stop "doing" certain tasks or begin more effectively managing their people-pleasing tendencies. Instead, they should begin focusing with greater intentionality on the hard work of rest as a discipline that not only restores their bodies but reorients them with a proper outlook on their true role in the kingdom of God.

The Discipline of Inactivity

My own wrestling with rest came by way of a young doctor in the rural town where I ministered. For weeks I struggled with a mysterious string of illnesses that left me aching, exhausted, and bedridden. I had not yet reached my thirtieth birthday, and my bloodwork looked like that of a man twice my age. "It might be leukemia," the doctor said somberly. After a second opinion, thankfully, it became clear that the leukemia was a false scare. But it was also clear that my current lifestyle was literally killing me. I call it a lifestyle, but that is purely a socially acceptable way of referring to what really was a disorder, a frenetic drive fueled by a monstrous desire to matter. Biologically, the bloodwork revealed what could only be called an undefined supervirus. My body was fully depleted and rebelling against my attempts to keep going by forcefully shutting down. Spiritually, the diagnosis was far more serious. Like an ominous sacrament, the state of my body was an outward sign of a dark inward reality—*I was addicted to a search for importance.*

I was raised in a broken home along with years of an internal script that led to long-feared failure coming of age in the years after college. I married young following my junior year. We started adding children shortly after I began seminary. Before our tenth anniversary, I was a father to three young sons, a college chaplain, the pastor of a newly birthed church plant, and an alcoholic. I remember early in childhood consciously adopting a mantra that helped me survive turmoil that would consume so much of my youth: *You are not a statistic.* I learned then, intuitively most of all, that children from homes like mine were generally not the ones voted most likely to succeed. Try though I did to let the saying guide me into beating the odds stacked against me, alas, it did not work. As if filling a role in a play, I made the very choices my sacred mantra was supposed to safeguard me from. In my teens, I exemplified the central casting figure of a rebellious, promiscuous partier who disengaged from school. I was a caricature of everything I swore I would never become.

Having embraced Jesus following my freshman year of college, I assumed, as many do, that the demons who had chased me for years would finally, once and for all, be vanquished, incinerated into oblivion. They instead just changed their clothes. Coming of age without a father, I was now a father myself. Having witnessed a string of divorces in my upbringing, here I was trying to decipher the complexities of married life completely devoid of any healthy models in my past. I was deeply insecure, and both my perceived and actual inadequacies seemed to rear their heads daily. No longer was I the disobedient teenager engaged in the temporary comfort of escapism. In one form or fashion, I was a grown man who knew nothing other than to run from his responsibilities. And like many pastors, I finally found refuge in ministry. Something the late theologian Watchman Nee wrote in *Sit, Walk, Stand* remains a truth I need to hear often:

> Most Christians make the mistake of trying to walk in order to be able to sit but that is the reverse of the true order. Our natural reason says if we do not walk, how can we ever reach the goal? But Christianity is a queer business. If at the outset we try to do anything we get nothing; if we seek to attain something, we miss everything. For Christianity begins not with a big DO but with a big DONE.[22]

There are two types of people who can speak (or write) about rest, balance, and our need for Sabbath. There are those who practice it voluntarily and those compelled to practice it because not doing so has led to prior self-destruction. I am in the latter group. The lessons I have learned about the limits of my humanity have come through

God kindly allowing me to crash and burn. It doesn't feel good, but it is a gift that God would bring me to a point of surrender, clarity, and restoration.

Eugene Peterson has been a gem to me, and clearly countless others, in traversing these issues. He points to creation itself as a model for the gift of rest. In the business of our contemporary society (where our second question after meeting someone is almost always, "What do you *do*?"), we are easily tempted to view our need for rest as evidence of a broken world and humankind's fall from grace in the garden. And yet when we read the opening chapter of Genesis, a strange order of wording removes this option: "And there was *evening*, and there was *morning*—the first day. And there was *evening*, and there was *morning*—the second day." With our post-enlightenment minds, we have become convinced that the work of each day begins with *me*. The work starts when I get to the office, fire up my computer, make the phone call, send the text message, show up on the site, say the right words at the right time, teach my first lesson, diagnose my first patient, write my first paragraph, or whatever else *I do*. I am the initiator of activity. However, to the ancient Hebrew, work was always *initiated* by God and *entered* into by people. *The real work starts when we go to sleep.* Peterson writes,

> This is the Hebrew way of understanding *day*; it is not ours. . . . Day is the basic unit of God's creative work; evening is the beginning of that day. It is the onset of God speaking light, stars, earth, vegetation, animals, man, woman, into being. But it is also the time when we quit our activity and go to sleep. . . . The Hebrew evening/morning sequence conditions us to the rhythms of grace. We go to sleep, and God begins his work. As we sleep, he develops his covenant. We wake and are called out to participate in God's creative action. We respond in faith, in work. But always grace is previous. Grace is primary. We wake into a world we didn't make; into a salvation we didn't earn.[23]

Therefore, this pattern calls us into everyday rest, regularly and often, without apology. God invites us to partner with God, not primarily as equal co-laborers but as fully rested second stringers emerging from the bench after the Starter has already won the game. Our pride may not like to hear that we are less necessary than we hoped, but our souls delight in the freedom that the world was not built on our shoulders, nor does it stop spinning when we lay our heads down to sleep. In fact, that is precisely when the real work begins.

Stephen L. Woodworth is an Assistant Pastor at Christ Presbyterian Church in Clarkesville, Georgia. He holds the Doctor of Ministry (DMin) degree from Gordon-Conwell Theological Seminary.

Confronting the Myth of the Balanced Life

Jul Medenblik

"All I want is some balance in my life." I don't know when I first heard such a cry or said it myself, but this longing is presented as a kind of nirvana. "If only I could have a balanced life and be a balanced individual, then I would feel _____ or would be _____" (fill in the blanks). Here is my thesis: it is all a lie that can wreck you and inflict great harm upon the person God intends you to be. Why do we work in the first place? Some of us work to please God and follow a calling. Others work to build a self-image that only ever amounts to a poor substitute of the *imago Dei* in us. And still others hide from God and everybody else by working like their lives depend on it, working without the benefit of any kind of healthy boundaries. I appreciate the purpose of this collection and find myself needing to confess that some people have accused me of "overwork," and there are times when they were right. Guilty as charged. For more than forty years, Gallup has studied human strengths and created language around the thirty-four most common talents, resulting in an assessment to help people detect which of them are authentically their own. This mechanism of discovery has been translated into more than twenty languages and used in more than one hundred nations the world over. According to Strengths-Finder, I am an Achiever, which it identifies as my number one trait theme. The material summarizes this aspect of my life as follows:

> Your achiever theme helps explain your drive. Achiever describes a constant need for achievement. You feel as if every day starts at

zero. By the end of the day, you must achieve something tangible in order to feel good about yourself. And by "every day" you mean every single day—workdays, weekends, vacation. . . . Your relentless need for achievement might not be logical. It might not even be focused. But it will always be with you. As an Achiever, you must learn to live with the whisper of discontent.[1]

As a church planter for sixteen years in the Chicagoland area and now as a seminary president, I have sometimes looked back and considered what I have actually done that is worthwhile in yesteryear's ledger, and my internal measuring scale says, "Not much." On those days especially, I like to mow the lawn and do the laundry, which explains why I have been the one in our household who primarily does the laundry since my early days as a seminary student way back in 1991! Let's just say that I am a high-motor, high-energy type of person. I want to accomplish something by the end of the day, yes, even if it is a small household task. Friends and family members have tried to relieve what they see as the burden of my achiever leanings by telling me not to work so hard. Their words have no effect. What has worked is understanding how God has wired me and confronting the myth of the balanced life.

The answer to the real problem of overwork will not be found in any one essay, particularly if it does not address the individual—you. What may trigger your leaning toward overworking? What in your history has created so much pressure that you follow it from resting in God's goodness to filling the void in your heart with things other than God that will always fall short? In the end, you must do business with God for clarity about that. It is an important task that you avoid at your own peril. I was reared in a family and a culture where Proverbs 16:18 (in the King James English, of course) seeped into the way my parents praised me or rather did not praise me. "Pride goeth before destruction, and a haughty spirit before a fall" meant that I rarely heard my parents say they were proud of me for fear of setting me up for some later destruction. Maybe they thought they were proactively defending me from laziness or from becoming an ingrate or someone who was flippantly irresponsible, never taking life seriously. The absence of recognition of any achievement would drive some people to underperform, finding solace in the lowest common denominator, but, as you might imagine, it led me to work harder—even to this day. The arc of my life has been formed by my persistent twisting to meet an unknown, ever-fleeting level where I will, hopefully and finally, hear affirming and even prideful words about who I am. Everyone has demons to deal with, often connected to some past wound or lack. And at one time or another, most of us wrestle with becoming good at hiding those negative facets of our formation from others. I know some of mine. Do you know yours?

A key breakthrough for me was forgiving my parents. They never asked for it. They weren't even fully aware of how their silence at my report cards misshaped me over time. In time, I found it important to better appreciate that they could not give what they themselves never had. As I matured, I recalled the silence of my grandparents and how their own handling of Proverbs 16:18 became the legacy for forming my parents, who then passed this lesson down to me. That's how it happens. They were only doing what they knew to do (or not do). It forced me to confront both generational sin and generational shame. But it wasn't enough to look just at my grandparents and parents; I needed most of all to look at Jesus's cross. What did the cross mean for me and my parishioners in this area of life? It meant that I became increasingly aware of how the stories of my parishioners had also been impacted by the troubles of their lives, past and present. I remember one young woman who was raising four children and being supportive of her doctor husband while trying to uphold a glittering, utopic image of their family when she was downright exhausted. She was "overworking."

During our pastoral conversations, I learned that her parents always favored her younger brother. He was the prince, and she was clearly left out of the royal court. In words that I take now as inspiration from the Holy Spirit, I felt prompted to address her and pray for her as a daughter of the King. Even if her earthly parents did not recognize her in this way, I named the biblical reality that she was, is, and shall ever be a uniquely valued child of God through faith in Jesus Christ. She cried. She broke down. The words I delivered as a messenger of God were transformed into water for her parched soul.

Through such encounters, I came to see the beauty of pointing people to Jesus and observing the subsequent wonder of them being "re-parented" by the indwelling of the Holy Spirit, then able to fully live into their identity as children of the Most High. I now read the disciples' request for Jesus to teach them to pray and Jesus's response as a "re-parenting" of them. I don't know what exact images shaped their way of prayer or their approach to God, just that Jesus invited them to see God as "Abba." Whatever distance was present for the disciples between them and God, Jesus bridged the gap by planting the image of children climbing into the lap of a loving Father who hugged them as they shared their deepest joys, sorrows, and concerns. Even as I began surrendering to being "re-parented" by God the Father, I still had to deal with my being an Achiever. My testimony is that crooked sticks can still draw straight lines. But was I called to restrain my achieving ways or embrace that aspect of myself? This seemed to be the $1,000,000 question.

Let me share a little more about my Achiever classification according to Tom Rath's *StrengthsFinder*:

> It [being an Achiever] does have its benefits. It brings you the energy you need to work long hours without burning out. It is the jolt you can always count on to get started on new tasks, new challenges. It is the power supply that causes you to set the pace and define the levels of productivity for your work group. It is the theme that keeps you moving.[2]

Being an Achiever has a shadowy side, but that's not all. Sunny days shine there, too. God uses all facets of our lives to shape and mold us. God is the potter; we are the clay. God has seen fit to turn my crookedness into something that not only can be used but that—when harnessed correctly—actually benefits me and others. Knowledge of how God has wired me has helped me avoid, at times, the idols that others might desire me to carry. Mind you, I am not perfect, but God has used me and my being an Achiever for God's glory. In the summer especially, maybe you know what it is like to spot in the distance while driving what appears to be water covering the road, only for the image to disappear the closer you get. The heat and surface of the road create a reflection that makes the "water" appear and then disappear. The image of a "balanced life" is a goal to be pursued, but I have yet to meet a person who lives an absolutely balanced one. It seems to disappear the closer you get. Note: I did not say a "full" life, which Jesus does desire to give to us as noted in John 10:10.

Like you, I have sat through tons of presentations and sermons, forgetting more than I will ever know. Wayne Cordeiro spoke on the subject of "Dead Leader Running" in 2006, though, and it has stuck with me ever since. He is the founding pastor of New Hope Christian Fellowship in Honolulu, Hawaii. Call me cynical if you must, but if there is anywhere that living a balanced life sounds realistic, it ought to be Hawaii, one of the most beautiful, serene locations on the entire planet. Cordeiro shared about deep struggles in his life and the pressures that led to being the kind of leader who was possessed by his own production. He wasn't getting enough sleep, and with depleted serotonin, pure adrenaline was running the show, which, of course, is a big no-no. He recounted his psychologist's warnings:

> The problem is that adrenaline is designed for emergency use only. It's like those doors in a restaurant that when opened cause an alarm to sound. Our problem, though, is that we use these pathways designed for emergency use only, but no alarm sounds. Not at first, anyway. Should you continue to run on adrenaline, it will destroy your system. You will burn out sooner on the inside than you're able to see on the outside. The fuel of adrenaline that keeps your engines running in the beginning will turn on you and destroy you in the end.[3]

Because he ultimately chose to pursue vulnerability and authenticity, Cordeiro's testimony truly reshaped my life. He addressed three things: What drains your tank? What fills your tank? Can you live a fulcrumed life? He took the first two questions together, noting that we are all wired differently by God. Some are extroverts. Some are introverts. Some of us love to go to a party. Others think a night all by their lonesome is the best form of entertainment. Our lives are like an emotional tank. The tank gets filled by things and people we enjoy and drained by things and people we do not enjoy as much or merely endure or survive. Therefore, we need to know what fills and drains our lives and then make sure we do enough to fuel our tanks to serve and to share life with others. Truthfully, you cannot sufficiently care for others if you are running on fumes.

For me, these insights were freeing because they put into words why I find twenty minutes in a good bookstore more refreshing than two hours at a beach. My wife is another story. Any amount of time spent at the beach is a huge win that refills her tank, while someone like me never learned to swim and doesn't even like sand to begin with! It just doesn't do it for me. But again, this isn't about right or wrong. We are wonderfully made in God's sight and unique in parts of our construction. Another highlight from Wayne Cordeiro is best illustrated by holding a yardstick in one hand and balancing it on one finger. Balancing a yardstick on one finger is not easy. Balance is hard to come by. And if you do find it for a moment, you recognize how fleeting it is. The wind blows, you are distracted, or something else occurs that causes the yardstick to tilt to one side or the other, and the next thing you know, in a flash your brief balance is gone.

Imagine a pastor who has their schedule laid out for the upcoming week. Everything is in the correct order, neat and tidy, prepared with proper "balance." But then, the reality of the week unfolds. Someone dies and the funeral is scheduled for Friday. A baby is born, but there is a bit of trouble, leaving the parents pacing about the NICU, overjoyed, hopeful, and yet scared out of their mind all at once. A couple who has just started coming to the church calls to say that they would like to meet and learn more about how to join. On top of the ministry demands that can be as nonstop as an open fire hydrant, there are personal concerns and responsibilities. For example, your daughter is the lead in the school play, and you already promised weeks ago to be there on opening night. Now move this week to the week before Easter or the week before Christmas, and you see how overwhelming it can suddenly get. How well is the yardstick balancing? Not so good.

As an Achiever, I am quick to say, "Bring it on!" There was a time when, in facing three services on Palm Sunday, the Maundy Thursday service, the Good Friday Ministerial Community service, and then three more Easter Sunday services, I viewed it as a noble mountain to climb and loved the challenge. Others did not. For them, there was dread and disappointment like despair after a Holy Week filled, or rather overfilled, to that kind of capacity. I was in danger of burning out others, including my family. Cordeiro was once more helpful in introducing me to "fulcrumed" living. Instead of seeing my finger as the balance for the yardstick, I was asked to see that finger as a fulcrum moving back and forth depending on ministry activities and busyness. The challenge was to move the fulcrum. If church work was filling the schedule one week, could I let go and ensure that the next week more of my time and attention went to refreshment and family? Living without moving the fulcrum is a recipe for disaster, but living with intentional movement is life-giving. I had been living with edges of this "fulcrumed living" in different ways. As a pastor who once was asked to officiate at eight different weddings in a summer, I had already arranged not to be crushed by the scheduling demands. I made sure to do the bulk of the premarital counseling in advance. I also promised that the honorariums would go to my family, especially our children, as a partial "make-up" for all the times I had to be away for rehearsals, ceremonies, and receptions. Cordeiro helped to expand my approach to ministry so that I worked smarter and maybe with greater sensitivity and insight, knowing that working hard was already something I was preconditioned for.

There will always be busy times in ministry. That is a promise. How one moves from constant busyness into a rhythm of sustainability boils down to embracing wisdom. Moving the fulcrum is easier when you and I recognize that ministry belongs to God, and it is a privilege to serve. Idolatry has many forms. Serving in ministry is no antidote to idolatry. The only way to steward the gift of ministry well is to align ourselves to the Lord along the lines of our giftedness and talents and then to stay as close to God as possible, embracing checks and balances that will keep us on the cross-centered straight and narrow. I don't think Jesus lived a balanced life. He gave it all for us. At the same time, he left us a great example for how to navigate a life of service for the sake of the gospel. He knew how to say

"Yes," "No," and "Not yet" without apology. He avoided the idols of ministry by knowing who he was serving and why. With that reservoir of meaning and relationship, Jesus ran the race set before him. May we run ours with him.

Jul Medenblik is the president of Calvin Theological Seminary in Grand Rapids, Michigan. He holds the JD from the University of
Florida

Confessions of a Recovering Workaholic

Rob A. Culbertson

Hello, we've not met yet. My name is Rod Culbertson, and I am a recovering workaholic. There, I said it. Let me try again. My name is Rod Culbertson, and I am a workaholic in progress. Okay, one last time. My name is Rod Culbertson, and *I am still a workaholic.* However, maybe like you, I am learning to do better. I cannot pinpoint exactly when I became a workaholic. It wasn't in early childhood. I was mostly a quiet kid who played alone, but some school official chose to place me in advanced classes beginning in the eighth grade, and for the next four years I ended up being at the bottom of my high-performing, advanced peers. A workaholic would never allow that to happen. Schoolwork was not my passion. I lived in the shadow of my older, "straight-A" sister and would never quite rise to that challenge. In the long run, I finished 110th in a high school class of 730—not bad but not a shining product of extraordinary diligence.

I finished my assignments in an obligatory fashion, survived, and graduated. I did develop one addiction growing up, though, and that was to my idol—baseball. I played it all day long. Play was work. Practice was joy. I could easily throw a baseball against a couple of walls (facilitating different bounces) in my front and back yards for hours. I believed that if I practiced all the time, I could make it to the major leagues. That might have been a fantasy, but I was consumed with the idea. I loved the game and thought the game loved me. Although I could have walked on at the University of South Carolina as a sophomore, I was converted to Christ in my first year and that changed everything. But baseball and the self-idolatry accompanying it were indeed early signs of a disordered approach to work.

In coming to Christ, I was utterly transformed. Though not overnight, eventually my motivation was greatly impacted. I not only discovered that I was to do all things for the glory of God, which needed to include my studies, but also that since the world was God's world, being a Christian student simply meant I could study anything due to a fascination with God's creation. Studying became a passion. And serving Christ as a student, through the campus ministry of Cru, became a priority. My life was never the same. I put forty hours per week into my campus ministry involvement in my junior year while also excelling in my studies. Many years later in my career, I would take the *StrengthsFinder* assessment and discover that I was an "Achiever," which I now know also made it easier for me to be an idolater.

In time, I seemed to transfer my discipline spent practicing baseball to a discipline that left no stone overturned in my entire life. Even today, I cannot escape the thought that I might be wasting time that could produce an eternal impact. As a young Christian, I still remember reading Ephesians 5:15-16, "Look carefully then how you walk, not as unwise but as wise, *making the best use of the time*, because the days are evil" (ESV, emphasis mine). The King James Version says, "redeeming the time"—i.e., saving it for eternity. That is sobering! Structuring my life for "success before the Lord" was eventually animated by creating a weekly calendar or chart that accounted for every hour of every day that I was awake. I used that calendar for about twenty years, in college, through seminary, doing campus ministry, and then as a church planter and pastor in Clearwater, Florida. I looked ahead each week and planned accordingly.

Some of my schedule consisted of blocks of hours (such as three hours in the morning for sermon preparation), as opposed to knowing what I was going to do every hour. I had a friend in college who took his calendar so seriously that he charted out what he was going to do every fifteen minutes. Even to me, that felt a bit over the top! He was fanatical—I was reasonable, I thought. Just two years ago, I read through most of John Wesley's famous diaries, and guess what? He, too, accounted for every fifteen minutes of his day, recording notes every evening after the day was done. Maybe that is why God used him to change the world! But let's be honest; I'm not Wesley.

While in seminary, I studied entirely too much and hardly had much of a social or active fitness life. As I entered campus ministry, ultimately with Reformed University Fellowship or RUF, mine was a unique situation. I was called to work for a local church in a campus town and doing campus ministry full-time, but my call did not include the promise of an actual salary. I would have to raise my own funds. Now was a time to trust the Lord—and we did—but I had to do my part, i.e., work hard for everything. I traveled all over the state of Florida to raise money and easily worked eighty hours per week that first year ministering to students, fundraising, leading Bible studies, preaching, and creating newsletters to update our small donor base.

The Reverend Mark Lowrey, founder of RUF, provided superior training for the early campus ministers like me who were still learning. As he did for so many others, he became a mentor to me. He didn't ask us how many hours we were working, but surely he had a sense that everyone was probably working too hard and too much. I had ceased working eighty hours per week by that time, mostly because my wife had given birth to our first child. Nevertheless, the demands of new, exhausting work continued to prevail. Except for their contribution to secure sufficient funding, those eighty hours didn't help much. My first year on campus was a disaster. My ministry group split in two, and neither took my side. I made a lot of mistakes. As Mark spoke during that initial training session I attended, I felt humility and embarrassment. He looked at us sternly, knowing that we were overdoing it with our respective ministries. He then talked about how to maintain sanity in what God had called us to. He said that for those in full-time ministry, their job is never finished. Its demands will never let up. Even though the campus had natural breaks in its schedule, unless we chose a more mature path in the beginning, most of us would probably keep working far beyond what we should for a lifetime.

Mark said we should have a reasonable work schedule throughout the week, with fifty to sixty hours as the maximum number contributed to the ministry. If we went over that amount, his advice was to make ourselves take a break, even an extra day off if needed, especially after a long student conference or weekend retreat. We needed to compensate ourselves wherever we could to guard against working too much. He came up with that figure because back then, the normal professional work week was based on the expectation of forty hours of work. He further stated that ministry, as a profession, could never be completed in a forty-hour week. But he clarified that the reason he used fifty to sixty hours as a standard for a ministry week is that in the local church, a layperson—particularly a church officer—would be working a forty-plus hour work week, and in addition to that, his service to the church would potentially add another ten hours to his week. No church minister should work less hours per week than his officers are working in their combined marketplace jobs and their official church service.

Pastor Lowrey set a conscientious standard for the *minimum* number of hours a campus minister should work each week at fifty. Still, he stated clearly that the fifty to sixty was the same as the maximum number of hours per week. I, Rod Culbertson, the workaholic, needed to hear and heed his advice. That intervention helped affirm a resolve in me to stop working so much. Curiously, my fallback strategy was to return to my scheduling system and make myself accountable to it. In campus ministry, I could easily work twelve-hour days from Monday through Wednesday. I loved it, and then I had other tasks to complete Thursday and over the weekend, not to mention Sunday responsibilities, either with the church I attended or elsewhere. I also usually tried to study three hours every Saturday morning until that time was replaced with my children doing sports and other activities. Sometimes Saturday evenings would include entertaining students or other social and/or fun events. The hours added up quickly. But thankfully, I learned that if the hours appeared to be heading toward an overload, *I could intentionally try to cut back* or take it "easier" over the weekend. This proved to be a good habit to carry forward. It helped save me from my natural bent toward workaholism. Of course, ministers don't really have a weekend in the traditional sense. That is why I took Fridays off, almost without exception. After a long week—Sunday through Thursday—Friday was mine. Fridays free felt a bit like "the weekend." This practice was also true when I became a church planter/pastor—Fridays off. If any of my four children had a school or athletic event during the week, I could break away for many of those.

On a personal level, I made time, and still do, for a devotional life. My best quiet times were observed in the evening, usually after everyone was in bed. Though not work time for me, it was still important to give it a place in my schedule. I was also careful to set time aside with my wife. It was a huge help that she loved the ministry. Although I do endorse date nights for couples, we didn't really have those. We went out some, but we also spent a lot of time together just doing ministry (i.e., having people over to our home) and raising children. The one thing I think she wanted me to do more than I did was help when company was coming. I didn't do that enough, but I tried to clean up (I don't really cook) and help bathe the kids and put them to bed. I should also add that I am not a "yes" person. I can say "no" and maintain boundaries, mostly without guilt. Later in my career, I heard the man who preceded me as a professor of pastoral theology at Reformed Theological Seminary, the late Dr. Frank Kik, annually tell pastoral students, "*You* are not the messiah. *You* cannot save the world." This fact is obvious, isn't it? Yet we live as if everyone else's salvation or Christian walk is dependent on us as ministers. Even worse are ministers who have a martyr complex. They are willing to go the extra mile, meet every need and jump at every ministry opportunity, take on the most insurmountable tasks, and make the ultimate sacrifice of self (like Jesus, they think) for the people they love. Commendable. The question, however, should be how often do these messiah and martyr complexes regularly result in spiritual burnout, loss of health (ministers are notoriously out of shape and overweight), and loss of precious time with one's spouse and family? No one is saved from anything this way. It only causes problems, not solves them. The fire engine is barely cooled down before there is another crisis to solve or squash, and off goes the fire chief, much to the chagrin of his loved ones and to the detriment of his own well-being.

Finally, let me mention that workaholism in my life created stress that caused potentially debilitating health problems. Campus ministry was a great challenge in my day, during the 1980s. Every ministry at the University of Florida suffered. And although no one was watching me, internally I felt like they were. I did not want to fail. I didn't fail, but "small" was not a useful promotional buzzword to raise a salary, as you can hopefully understand. Nevertheless, because of my sense of responsibility—leading to my workaholism—I put undue pressure on myself. For three consecutive summers (1983–1985), the stress haunted me physically. First, I got mononucleosis. That laid me up for over two months that summer—I was absolutely worn out. I came down with shingles the next summer, completely stress related, which is not unusual. The third summer, I ran into a painful problem called TMJ (temporomandibular joint), in which your jaw comes out of the joint while you sleep. Again, stress related. Often surgery or an expensive custom mouthpiece is required. I had a consultation with a world-renowned TMJ expert at the University of Florida. He mentioned one nonsurgical option that might work: stop worrying. He said, "As a minister, you probably have a lot of stress in your life. You need to stop being anxious about those problems." Oh my! He may as well have been quoting Philippians 4:6-7 to me, and in many ways he was. I had created my own idol once again—ME. I wasn't trusting God. As I drove away from Shands Teaching Hospital that afternoon, I prayed, "Lord, I am going to give this ministry to you and not carry the burden like I have been doing. Even if I fail, it's yours." I had a settled peace that day, and although I still get and feel stressed out at times, I have come to understand the need to let God do the work while I work for God. I lasted in campus ministry for another five years. A few years later, I created a short slogan that defines the Christian life for me today and keeps me mostly free from workaholism: "Rest in His work. Work in His rest."

If nothing else did, I hope the following counsel inspires you to think differently about workaholism in ministry:

1. Set boundaries for your ministry and the time you spend in it.

2. Make fellowship with God a priority. Jesus, as busy as he was and even being the Son of God, took what appear to be breaks—or vacations—in his ministry. He "fled" the demands of the crowds at times, and he also spent private time with his heavenly Father in prayer. It feels inconceivable, but he escaped to be alone with God, so we must as well.

3. Beware of adopting an opposite extreme. The flip side of the "workaholic" issue could be creating another form of idolatry, that of apathy or laziness. A minister could make cherishing his family, as well as his leisure, such a protected priority that the ministry does not receive the attention God expects it to receive. Ministry is not a place of ease, and you must live in the tension of both working conscientiously and loving your spouse and family. If pastors are "worthy of their hire," then they must work for that worthiness as well as for the compensation promised to them for their labors.

4. Value your spouse. Not everyone in ministry is married, but if you are, don't take your spouse for granted. Investing in this primary relationship is, in my opinion, more important than your ministry. Ministries and ministers come and go, but marriage partners should not, especially because ministry has usurped their rightful place. We all hate adultery. However, there is a lesson here: the church can be your mistress, tempting you to love her first. She can rob you of the love for your spouse that would normally bloom in time as longevity and intimacy thrive in your marriage. Don't let workaholism capture your heart.

May you grow in God's grace to trust God for what you ultimately can't make happen anyhow. May you find pleasure in God's service. May you rest assured that God is walking alongside you all the way.

Rod A. Culbertson is the Dean of Student Development and an Associate Professor of Pastoral Theology at Reformed Theological Seminary in Charlotte, North Carolina. He holds the Doctor of Ministry (DMin) degree from Reformed Theological Seminary.

Time Alone: Discovering My Identity

David Sherbino

"I think I will quit and find something else to do." These thoughts were running through my mind after a year in pastoral ministry. As a recent theological graduate, I was eager to serve in the church and jumped into ministry with excitement and determination. Doing well and succeeding have always been driving forces in my life, and the motto I lived by was "work hard and get ahead." Consequently, at the end of this first newfound year in ministry, I was emotionally, spiritually, and physically drained. The fresh programming was exciting, and yes, the number of participants had grown, but there were nagging questions in the back of my mind. "How do I keep up this pace?" "What do I do next year and the following year?" "How much is enough?" I hoped a summer vacation and break from ministry's insistent daily demands would renew me so I could reengage well later.

While I vacationed at a cottage, the opportunity arose one evening to go to dinner at a conference center across the lake. A chapel service was scheduled, but I had no interest in another "church event" while trying to relax away from ministry. However, when I learned the speaker was the moderator of the Presbyterian Church in Ireland, my intrigue piqued. He was from the same tradition I related to, and the Irish are known as great storytellers. What was there to lose? So I went. At the conclusion of the service, I introduced myself to the speaker. During our conversation, he asked me a simple, straightforward question: "Do you like congregational ministry?" I told him that I found ministry demanding, draining, and not as nearly fulfilling as anticipated. He seemed to understand, but instead of giving me a spiritual pep talk, he asked a second question: "How is your relationship with God?" Somewhat caught off-guard, I mumbled something about, "It seems to be okay." "Oh," he replied, "I have discovered that many in ministry become discouraged and depleted when they are not spending time alone with God."

I was busy, and from a ministry perspective all the metrics looked good. I knew one thing was lacking, however—the nurturing of my relationship with God. But when life is busy, the demands never-ending, and ministry and the ensuing success are the basis of one's identity, how can you find time to nurture your soul? You simply keep going, even if you are on the verge of burnout. I was familiar with the statement used by Christian leaders who declared they would rather "burn out than rust out." But as I reflected on this statement, it became clear to me that in the final analysis, either way you were "out." The only difference is one process takes a bit longer than the other. And that is no way to live. Sadly, many Christians believe being busy doing "spiritual" things should be the focus of one's spirituality. New Testament professor Bruce Demarest wrote,

> The badge of busyness we so proudly wear is a demon of our times. Our competitive, "survival of the fittest" culture is unabashedly performance driven. And so, we are in the church. We find our identity and measure our worth in what and how much we accomplish. . . . Listening to God? Whatever for? . . . Learning to be open and directable, isn't that a waste of time? Learning to "rest" our spirits in God—isn't that an excuse for not obeying God? The demon of busyness whispers in our ears, also blinding our eyes to the fact that our pressured lives leave us irritable, uncaring, vulnerable, and guilt-ridden when we see that we haven't accomplished everything on our spiritual "to do" list. Compassion grows numb, God gets put on hold, and the flesh quenches the Spirit.[1]

Busyness as a measure of one's spirituality is not new in the least. In Jesus's day, many people were entangled in religious activity and missed out on what was truly essential. Jesus said, "Many will say to me on that day, 'Lord, Lord, did we not prophesy in your name and in your name drive out demons and, in your name, perform many miracles?' Then I will tell them plainly, 'I never knew you'" (Matt 7:22-23, NIV). The people Jesus referred to were busy folks engaged in ministry and doing good things. Despite all their effort, though, they neglected to build a vibrant, intimate relationship with God. They missed out!

We know that a relationship with God is the most important component in life, but it can only happen when we are open and present to the One who is always available to us and is a present help. We are reminded of the psalmist's invitation and instruction from Psalm 46:10: "Be still and know that I am God." Most people do not desperately need more theological knowledge about God. What they need is a life empowered to obey God developed from an intimate relationship with God. For such a relationship to occur, one must make space and time for God. The spiritual practice of solitude is where we begin. Henri Nouwen wrote, "Without solitude it is virtually impossible to live a spiritual life. Solitude begins with a time and place for God and God alone."[2] For most people, the practice of solitude is not easy. We live in a culture that views this as unproductive time, and, conversely, we applaud and reward the busyness and accomplishments of people. Author and spiritual director Ruth Haley Barton writes in *Sacred Rhythms: Arranging Our Lives for Spiritual Transformation*,

> The practices of silence and solitude are radical because they challenge us on every level of our existence. They challenge us on the level of culture: there is little in Western culture that supports us in entering what feels like unproductive time for being and listening. They confront us on the level of our human relationships: they call us away from those relationships for a time so we can give undivided attention to God. They challenge us on the level of our soul: in the silence we become aware of inner dynamics we have been able to avoid by keeping ourselves noisy and busy.[3]

Retreat director and spiritual director Stephen Smith reinforces the idea that simply engaging in various activities and being busy does not develop a close relationship with God. He declares, "A life of prolonged busyness, engaging with people, performing tasks, and expanding your knowledge about God does not help you experience God. More information, no matter how good it is, does not yield a transformed life. Transformation and deep change are ushered in by experiencing God, not just knowing about God. And stillness is required."[4]

Jesus regularly employed the spiritual practice of solitude. Before beginning his public ministry, he was led into the desert wilderness for forty days to fast and pray in silence and solitude (Matt 4:1-11). In this place he was alone, hungry, hot, and thirsty and tested by Satan. It would be a time of preparation for the ministry assignment his Father had for him, and it was an assignment unlike no other—to save humankind. At the conclusion of this forty-day period of solitude, Matthew records three different temptations Jesus encountered, which were intended to entice him not only away from his assignment but also away from his identity. The three temptations Jesus faced are the same ones that will challenge every follower of Jesus, but especially those in leadership need to make note of them. The first temptation was to be relevant: "If you are the Son of God, turn these stones into bread" (Matt 4:3). In ministry we face this similar temptation. Nouwen states,

> Are we not all called to do something that makes a difference in people's lives? Aren't we called to heal the sick, feed the hungry and alleviate the suffering of the poor? Jesus was faced with the same questions, but when he was asked to prove his power as the Son of God by the relevant power of changing stones into bread, he clung to his mission to proclaim the word and said, "human beings live not by bread alone but by every word that comes from the mouth of God."[5]

Perhaps in our attempt to be relevant, we work hard at trying to meet all the needs and wants of people. We may even have a need to be needed. Nouwen challenges us to be careful and to be aware of this subtle temptation. For Nouwen, the "leader of the future will be one who dares to claim his irrelevance in the contemporary world as a divine vocation that allows him or her to enter into a deep solidarity with the anguish underlying all the glitter of success and to bring the light of Jesus there."[6]

The second temptation Jesus faced was to be spectacular or popular, to do something that would win the approval and applause of the crowd. "If you are the Son of God, throw yourself down from the highest pinnacle. . . . He will command his angels concerning you, and they will lift you up in their hands so that you will not strike your foot against a stone" (Matt, NIV 4:6). Nouwen states,

> Jesus refused to be a stuntman. He did not come to prove himself. . . . When you look at today's Church, it is easy to see the prevalence of individualism among ministers and priests. Not too many have a vast repertoire of skills to be proud of. But most of us feel that if we have anything at all to show, it is something we have to do solo. . . . Stardom and individual heroism, which are such obvious aspects of our competitive society, are not at all alien to the Church. There too the dominant image is that of the self-made man or woman who can do it all alone.[7]

The third temptation was the temptation of power. "Again, the devil took him to a very high mountain and showed him all the kingdoms of the world and their splendor. 'All this I will give to you if you bow down and worship me'" (Matt 4:8-9). Nouwen writes,

> One of the greatest ironies of the history of Christianity is that its leaders constantly give in to the temptation of power. . . . The temptation to consider power an apt instrument for the proclamation of the Gospel is the greatest of all. We keep hearing from others, as well as saying to ourselves, that having power—provided it is used in the service of God and your fellow human beings—is a good thing. With this rationalization crusades took place; inquisitions were organized; . . . much moral manipulation of conscience was engaged in. What makes the temptation of power so seemingly irresistible? Maybe it is that power offers an easy substitute for the hard task of love. It seems easier to be God than to love God, easier to control people than to love people, easier to own life than to love life. One thing is clear; the temptation of power is the greatest when intimacy is a threat. Much Christian leadership is

exercised by people who do not know how to develop healthy, intimate relationships and have opted for power and control instead. Many Christian empire-builders have been people unable to give and receive love.⁸

Jesus did not succumb to these temptations, but that did not mean the enemy was finished with him. Facing temptation would be an ongoing reality. Jesus regularly withdrew from the busyness and demands of life and ministry to be quiet and alone with the Father (Mark 1:35; Luke 6:12; 22:39-46). This is how he remained focused, renewed, and empowered.

In ministry, there is the constant temptation to be relevant, popular, and powerful. We might not openly admit it, many have developed a lifestyle and ministry focused on what they accomplish and how others regard them because that has become the basis of their identity. I refer to this identity as one that is "performance oriented." In other words, I am accepted, approved, and applauded based on how well I do. Consequently, there is an internal drive to accomplish more and more, which for many in ministry can lead to emotional burnout and disillusionment. The hard question to ask is do I believe my identity is based on what I do or who I am? If I believe my identity is based on what I do, not only will I keep working to prove myself, but I will be living out of my false self. Theologian Richard Rohr writes, "Our false self is who we think we are. It is our mental self-image and social agreement, which most people spend their whole lives living up to or down to."⁹

Living out of the false self requires a lot of energy. There is the constant comparison, the desire for more, the fixation on meeting the needs and demands of others to please them and win their approval. In the church setting, this can mean building bigger budgets, growing congregations, offering a greater variety of programs, and at the same time being available to everyone at any time. Basil Pennington states it succinctly: ". . . the false self . . .is made up of what I have, what I do, and what others think of me."¹⁰ All of this runs counter to what God says about our identity. Jesus's identity was based on knowing who he was. At his baptism heaven opened, the Spirit of God descended on him like a dove, and a voice from heaven said, "This is my Son, whom I love; with him I am well pleased" (Matt 3:17). The declaration that Jesus was the "beloved of God" was the essence of his identity, and this was known by him before he began his public ministry. Jesus's identity was not based on what he did. Rather it was centered on his relationship with the Father. Out of this relationship, knowing he was loved by the Father, Jesus would minister to people and carry out the assignment the Father had given to him. The questions each person needs to consider are, "Do you know you are the beloved of God? Is this the basis of your identity?" If you believe it is, you will not be driven in ministry by your compulsions/temptations to be relevant, popular, and powerful as the essence of who you are. However, if you believe your identity is revealed by what you do, you will become exhausted and disillusioned trying to achieve that reality.

This does not mean your life will not be busy and demanding, but if you know your identity as the "beloved of God," you will have a different perspective. As Jesus engaged in ministry, he did not run here and there to meet the needs of people. Often, he withdrew from the busyness of life and ministry to be alone with God. In those times of solitude, he was able to be renewed and to listen and discern what God was asking of him. In the opening chapter of Mark's Gospel, we are given a brief insight into a day in the life of Jesus and how he took time out of a demanding schedule to be in solitude. It was the Sabbath, and Jesus was teaching in the synagogue. While he was teaching, a demonized man began to cry out, and Jesus casted the evil spirit out. Upon finishing teaching, Jesus went to the house of Simon ,whose mother-in-law was ill, and the woman her from her sickbed. After supper, the whole town gathered at Simon's place, and Jesus healed those who were sick or demon possessed. By all accounts, he had a busy day ministering to the needs of people! The next morning while it was still dark, Jesus went to a solitary place to pray. There was no one with him, and he was free from all distractions to be alone with his Father. When his disciples eventually found him, they wanted Jesus to go with them to minister to the crowds in the town, but Jesus did not give in to their request. He chose to go elsewhere. He knew what he was to do and was not pressured or led by the demands of others.

How did Jesus know when to say yes and when to say no to the requests of others? This knowledge would be important, for throughout his life many people would make constant demands of him. Peter Scazzero, a retired pastor and successful author, suggests that some wanted a Messiah who would feed them, some wanted a Messiah to fix all their problems, some wanted a Messiah to overthrow the Roman oppressors, and some wanted a Messiah who would be their miracle worker.[11] Despite these competing voices, Jesus was not distracted by them because his ministry was not based on being liked by others. His ministry was not based on trying to be relevant, nor was his ministry based on trying to gain power. His only desire was to do his Father's will. In places of silence and solitude, Jesus was able to listen and hear the voice of the Father, and as he discerned what the Father desired, this became the path he followed. Jesus could confidently and accurately confess, "I always do what pleases him" (John 8:29). Obedience to the voice of God was central to his life and ministry, and at the end of his ministry Jesus could say, "I have finished the work that you gave me to do" (John 17:4). Without solitude and silence, life can become destructive because we then cling to the results of our work and ministry as a way of self-identification. Nouwen states that

> in solitude we can slowly unmask the illusion of our possessiveness and discover in the center of our own self that we are not what we can conquer but what is given to us. In solitude we can listen to the voice of the One who spoke to us before we could speak a word, who healed us before we could make any gesture to help, who set us free long before we could free others, and who loved us long before we could give love to anyone. It is in this solitude that we discover that being is more important than having, and that we are worth more than the results of our efforts.[12]

Ministry may be demanding and stressful, but there is a peace that flows from being in the presence of God. In that solitary place, God will renew and refresh you and enable you to fully embrace life.

Jesus said, "Come to me all who are weary and burdened, and I will give you rest. Take my yoke upon you and learn of me for I am gentle and humble of heart, and you will find rest for your souls. For my yoke is easy and my burden is light" (Matt 11:28-30). Solitude is an important practice that is not to be entered into lightly. We are so accustomed to noise and activity that we wonder how we will cope if we enter solitude. Solitude may bring to the surface inner conflict, distress, longings, or temptations that can be so challenging we may try to avoid or ignore these issues by staying busy. With one being a psychologist and one a theologian, Siang-Yang Tan and Douglas Gregg believe that in solitude we can be purged of perverted desires and given a clearer perception of ourselves and others. In *Disciplines of the Holy Spirit: How to Connect to the Spirit's Power and Presence*, they write,

> The Holy Spirit is given time and space to speak to us and we are given time and space to hear his voice. The Holy Spirit dwells in us, providing the power to overcome temptation and transform our testing, strengthening us for the battles ahead. We emerge out of times of solitude with a better understanding of our strengths and weaknesses and a deeper love and affection for God, our protector and defender.[13]

Dallas Willard only reinforces the idea that solitude is challenging and difficult and claims "we can only survive solitude as we cling to Christ there."[14] But as you cling to Christ, you will discover that his presence is a place of grace, and that is more than enough.

If the Son of God regularly engaged in solitude, we also need to embrace it as an essential practice. There are basic steps to consider as you begin this journey of time alone with God. Some might rise early in the morning when all is quiet, before the demands of the day begin, and spend time with God. If you prefer the evening, then make that your time of solitude. Whatever time you choose, it is important to be free from all distractions that would redirect your focus away from God. There may be brief interludes during your day when you can focus on a Bible verse or repeat a breath prayer. If you are traveling alone in your vehicle, use that time to be in solitude with God.

Turn off the radio or podcast, acknowledge the presence of God, and listen for God's voice. Finally, you might schedule a day away once a month to spend an extended period with God without any agenda other than being in God's presence. It is here you are reminded that you are "the beloved," and it is here you are aware of God's presence as you go about the tasks of the day. Without the spiritual practice of solitude, life will be frantic, and our lives will feel impoverished. According to Nouwen, "Solitude is not simply a means to an end; solitude is its own end. It is the place where Christ remodels us in his own image and frees us from the victimizing compulsions of the world. Solitude is the place of our salvation."[15]

David Sherbino is a Professor of Spirituality and Pastoral Ministry and also the Doctor of Ministry Spiritual Formation Track Coordinator at Tyndale Seminary in Canada's Toronto, Ontario. He holds the Doctor of Ministry (DMin) degree from Fuller Theological Seminary.

Turning Down the Volume on Demands

Kyle Denny

"Everyone is looking for you" (Mark 1:37). There is not enough time. Short and sweet is how most would describe our problem. In a pastor's world, there are twenty things that need to be accomplished, and we have time for three or four of them. Thus, we have a mounting temptation to overwork ourselves. This isn't unique to ministry. When working in public accounting, I felt a similar force, but in the church, we have a special ability to justify our job's unhealthy habits. We tell ourselves, "I'm not working to store up earthly riches; I'm shepherding God's flock," or "I'm the only one who can do it." God has called us to this, after all. We start fantasizing about how if we only had a few more hours each day, we could fit everything in. If we were a little more effective with our email responses or if people would just quit interrupting, then, by gosh, we could get it all done. This is building up a straw man, however: the problem of overwork has never been the twenty-four-hour restriction of time or how seriously we take our jobs. The true problem lies in the lens through which we see our obligations. It's a slight derailment in our thinking that steers us astray. We gorge ourselves on the idol of self.

Moses: Our Example

Truly, there is nothing new under the sun. The lie that spawns overwork has been infiltrating the minds of leaders for millennia. Moses stumbled into it when he first led Israel out of Egypt. He sat down to judge the people, and from morning until evening people stood around him as he tried to help them. Can you imagine his exhaustion? He's sitting in the day's heat, emotionally bearing all kinds of burdens, carefully listening, and he never makes a dent in the work to be done. In fact, it's likely that the line of people who need his help grows longer by the hour. He knows he must settle the people's problems and teach them about God, and so in good faith he proceeds the only way he knows how: working hard alone. That seems to be a leader's natural reaction. I'll skip dinner and tell my partner I'll be late because this work is too important to leave unfinished. Thankfully, this is not the example God approves for our ministry.

Moses's father-in-law, Jethro, happens to be around too, and God gives him the wisdom and boldness to proclaim, "What you are doing is not good" (Exod 18:17). I often wonder if that was hard for Moses to hear. I wouldn't be surprised if he was thinking, "I'm worn dangerously thin, trying to do God's work. What do you mean, 'what I'm doing is not good'? I'm doing the *best* I can." If that was on his mind, the text never alludes to it. For Moses, wounds from a friend heal. Jethro foresees the burnout not only for the leader but also for the followers. Moses will be overly burdened, and his ability to help the people will be greatly diminished, so he gives Moses some much-needed counsel: "If you do this, God will direct you, you will be able to endure, and all these people also will go to their place in peace" (Exod 18:23). What crucial advice will help turn the tide of exhaustion and burnout? The instructions are both simple and hard: Share the load. You cannot carry it alone.

Is your heart pushing back at this? Are you already defending why you must work such long hours? Are you thinking, "That's easy to say, but you don't know my situation"? It's true, I don't. I also don't pretend to. I'm not someone who stands on the opposite shore cheering you on but rather a fellow co-laborer and shepherd struggling through the river's current himself, at times choking on mouthfuls of water. I'm still working through how this can go better in my life, but things cannot improve if we deny that we are responsible for the problem and have agency to recalibrate our approach. There are others able to do the work of God. The church is meant to build itself up in love, not to be built up through my efforts alone.

Whatever it looks like, however it takes shape, there is no avoiding that we need to share the load. That sounds a bit naive, doesn't it? We'd love to share the load—there's just no one qualified or willing to contribute to that degree. That's why there is a second component of the problem. We believe that we shall not, indeed cannot disappoint people. But Jesus saw right through that lie, and he faced the consequences of it daily.

Jesus Disappointed People

Mark 1 recounts, among other things, how sought after Jesus was. He taught in such a way and with such authority that throngs of people were regularly amazed. His healing and miracles eventually brought people to him by the thousands. We see that the whole city of Capernaum was gathered at his door on one occasion, waiting for him to heal those sick with diseases and free those enslaved to demon possession (Mark 1:33). It appears to be going according to the people's expectation until, under the cover of darkness, Jesus rises early in the morning and abruptly leaves to pray in isolation. His disciples eventually find him here and tell him, "Everyone is looking for you" (Mark 1:37). Do you ever feel like that—like you simply can't get a moment of peace? Well, Jesus's response surprised me. Instead of going back and explaining to those people that he had to move on and why, he says, "Let us go on to the next towns, that I may preach there also, for that is why I came out" (Mark 1:38). Can you imagine the disappointment this caused? I cringe just thinking about it. Jesus stirred up an entire city and left. They were looking for Jesus, and he didn't even tell them he was leaving. It comes across a little rude, doesn't it? Yet that was the best thing Jesus could do because it's the very thing Jesus did. Disappointing people is not sinful. It goes without saying that it should not be our goal, but sometimes it is unavoidable. It's a fact of life that we will disappoint and be disappointed. These people had expectations. They had their own views on what was right and what should be done, but God's way was better, as always. God's reality was different than what they thought it would be. More importantly, Jesus was not a slave to their approval. He had an iron-clad grasp on what his mission was. He was wise enough not to burden himself with their ill-informed, manipulative expectations, so he left. Praise God.

If you are anything like me, that's hard. People-pleasing feels tightly enmeshed with my DNA somehow. But while I want to help people as best as I can, at the end of the day I want to follow God wherever God leads. Jesus loved people far better than I ever will, and part of the way he did this was choosing to disappoint them rather than abandon his Father's work. To share the load, we must allow others to fill the gap. This will always lead to some discontentment, but we must learn to embrace it as Jesus did. It is hard to care for people holistically anyway if you are doing it out of fear, so most of us need to deconstruct why we live and work as pastors the way we do. Does it please God, or does it seek to please our own ego or what others unfairly expect of us?

The Process

We need to share the load, even though it might lead to hurt feelings, dissatisfaction, and criticism. The next practical question is, "How?" Returning to Moses and Jethro, we see specific instructions. In Exodus 18:21-22, Jethro says,

> Moreover, look for able men from all the people, men who fear God, who are trustworthy and hate a bribe, and place such men over the people as chiefs of thousands, of hundreds, of fifties, and of tens. And let them judge the people at all times. Every great matter they shall bring to you, but any small matter they shall decide themselves.

Even if these instructions aren't applicable to us in the detail provided (i.e., I certainly don't need chiefs of thousands), we can still extract two main ideas. We need to find other leaders and give them the freedom to handle the small things that bog us down. The leaders should be "able." This word in Hebrew carries the idea of a person's ability or quality. This is not directly about skills: those are important, but they can be learned if a person is "able." This quality, combined with the fear of God, trustworthiness, and righteousness, is what we should look for in a leader. Once we find someone, we need to give them proper training and then freedom to grow. To share the load doesn't mean we pastors abandon the load. There's still a responsibility to oversee the leaders and certain projects, but it leaves room for our core responsibilities. Jesus is an even better fulfillment of this than Moses. Even though he is God, and fully capable of doing everything himself, we see him time and time again affirm this method. Logically, that makes sense because he's the embodiment of Wisdom, and God doesn't change. Jesus chose apostles who met this criterion (except Judas, but that's a different story entirely). They were able men who feared God. They were trustworthy.

Hiccups and Disappointments

We see Jesus giving his followers enormous freedom to work. During his earthly ministry, he allowed the apostles, and some select disciples, to have authority over illness and demons, and he sent leaders out to do the Father's work. Jesus trusted them with "small matters," relatively speaking. While we see many hiccups along the way—like that little incident where James and John wanted to annihilate a Gentile town with fire from above—I want to focus on a specific, impactful fiasco.

Jesus is returning with Peter, James, and John from his Transfiguration and happens upon a chaotic scene. Scribes are arguing with his disciples, and a huge crowd has formed around them, so Jesus asks for an explanation, maybe in a similar way that I do with my two-year-old son. But before details can be articulated, we hear a father's voice pipe up in the crowd (Mark 9:17). Apparently, this father had brought his demon-possessed son to the disciples for healing, but they couldn't do it, which understandably led to a tense situation. The father is fatalistic, the scribes are combative, and the disciples are discouraged and confused. There's plenty of disappointment to go around.

This will happen in our pastoral lives, too. When we find people to fill the gap, disappointment will follow. It isn't a matter of *if* but of *when* and *how*. It works exactly how Jethro described it: "small matters" hit a snag and get kicked back up the ladder. We see Jesus step in, and it becomes a powerful teaching moment for his ragtag crew of disciples. Wouldn't you know it—prayer was the only thing that could drive out that kind of demon. We can point fingers at the disciples, immaturely snickering at their audacity to try to remove demons without prayer, but it had worked for them until then, so they probably surmised that what isn't broken doesn't need fixing. The disappointing situation turned into a lesson they wouldn't soon forget. This is one example of Jesus's arduous battle in training his leaders. They were hardened and without the Spirit. They were influenced heavily by culture and so, like us today, were constantly misunderstanding Jesus. Regardless, he chose them and empowered them. Jesus willingly meets people in the muck, where they are, and slowly walks with them through it.

Impossible Things

Sometimes, Jesus asks us—yes, you and me—to do truly impossible things. Pastoral overwork is our attempt to serve God in our strength, which will never be enough. In John 6, when Jesus is sitting on a mountain, he sees a whole swarm of people in the distance. A large crowd of at least 5,000 are slowly making their way towards him. As he watches their approach, he asks Philip where they could buy bread to feed them. Philip, without skipping a beat, replies incredulously that $40,000 (my humble approximation) wouldn't be enough to give each of them even a little. What an impossible task. And yet, do you wonder why Jesus put it on his disciples in the first place? He's God. He already knows what he's going to do. Why befuddle them with a misleading question? He's not going to buy food at all. The incredible things we find in our ministry are not a test of our own strength; they are an invitation to witness Jesus's strength. They serve as an invitation to greater dependence. Pastoral overwork substitutes our reliance on God for reliance on self. It is a short-term and sinful solution stoking the fire of a long-term problem that is always more monstrous than we think. Philip could only see what Jesus was asking him to do, which was feed all those people. He never slowed down enough to imagine and trust that Jesus had something in mind that would be altogether different from anything he could concoct.

You may face sizable barriers in raising leaders or in shifting how you work. But rest assured that God is not a cruel taskmaster. God is a loving Father. Maybe the answer isn't to work in your own strength but to pause, embrace new rhythms, and ask what God's got in mind.

Where Is the Line?

To end, I need to clear the air and acknowledge that I wrestle a lot with where the line is for pastoral overwork. I know we're called to a substantial and holy task that we don't take lightly. We are expected to keep watch over the flock (Acts 20:28), and we will one day give an account to God for them (Heb 13:17). We will be judged more strictly because of our teaching (Jas 3:1). The senior pastor I serve under describes this weight as "the things that keep you up in the middle of the night." But in the same way that we're to keep an eye on the flock and care for them, we're first to keep an eye on ourselves. If my ministry for the local church succeeds but my marriage or my family blows up because I have neglected one or both, then was I really caring for myself the way I should have? I doubt it. With that said, I don't have a cookie-cutter answer for where everyone's line should be. For some it may be fifty hours, and for others it may be more, but I know there are limits for each of us that we desperately need to work within. We aren't pastoral superheroes. We have limits. There are times we will need to answer emergency calls in the middle of the night or give counsel during unexpected and inconvenient moments. There are times we will have to miss life with our family and friends. There are times we will feel worn incredibly thin. When that becomes the norm, however, instead of the exception, we know we have begun wading into dangerous waters.

Kyle Denny is the Youth Pastor and Finance Director at New Hope Church in East Lansing, Michigan.

Endnotes

Chapter 1 — Making the Best of a Day Off

1. Craig C. Hill, *Servant of All: Status, Ambition, and the Way of Jesus* (Grand Rapids, MI: Eerdmans, 2016), 177.

2. Ibid.

3. Ibid.

Chapter 3 — "What you Are Doing Is Not Good": Exodus 18 and Pastoral Overwork

1. Cf. Wynne Davis, "You Don't Have To Be An Olympian To Prioritize Your Mental Health," *NPR Online*, May 28, 2021, https://www.npr.org/2021/07/28/1021668310/mental-health-simone-biles-olympics.

2. E.g., Edwin Chr. Van Driel, "What Is Jesus Doing?: Christological Thoughts for an Anxious Church and Tired Pastors," in *What Is Jesus Doing? God's Activity in the Life and Work of the Church*, ed. Edwin Chr. Van Driel (Downers Grove, IL: Intervarsity, 2020), 1–26; L. Roger Owens, "Shaping a Pastoral Spirituality," in *What Is Jesus Doing?* 135–56; L. Roger Owens, "Staying with God: Eugene Peterson and John Chapman on Contemplation," in *Pastoral Work: Engagements with the Vision of Eugene Peterson*, ed. Jason Byassee and L. Roger Owens (Cascade Press, 2014), 131–42; Andrew Purves, *The Crucifixion of Ministry: Surrendering Our Ambitions to the Service of Christ* (Downers Grove, IL: Intervarsity, 2002); Parker J. Palmer, *Let Your Life Speak: Listening for the Voice of Vocation* (San Francisco: Jossey-Bass, 2000); Marianne Bernhard, "Clergy Burnout: When Stress, Overwork Overwhelm the Spirit," *Washington Post*, May 7, 1981, https://www.washingtonpost.com/archive/local/1981/05/08/clergy-burnout-when-stress-overwork-overwhelm-the-spirit/4a628f77-e9e4-4c76-b329-ad61977fac64/.

3. Unless otherwise noted, Scripture quotes in this essay are from the NRSV. Much of what follows is drawn from my work in "God Redeems a People," *Adult Bible Studies Teacher* (Nashville: United Methodist Publishing House, Summer 1994), 41–45.

4. With, e.g., Jeffrey Tigay, "Exodus: Introduction and Notes," in *The Jewish Study Bible*, 2nd ed., ed. Adele Berlin and Marc Zvi Brettler (Oxford: Oxford University, 2014), 134; William H. C. Propp, *Exodus 1–18: A New Translation*

With Introduction and Commentary, AYB 2 (New York: Doubleday, 1998), 627; and Richard Elliott Friedman, *Who Wrote the Bible?* (New York: Harper & Row, 1987), 251. Brevard Childs (The Book of Exodus: A Critical and Theological Commentary, OTL [Louisville: Westminster, 1974], 321) notes that, while "most commentators assign the chapter to E," it is more important to consider the chapter as a whole in its canonical context; so too John I. Durham, Exodus, WBC 3 (Waco, TX: Word, 1987), 245. John Van Seters, who rejects the hypothesis of an E source (cf. The Pentateuch, Trajectories 1 [Sheffield: Sheffield Academic, 1999], 59), ascribes the passage to his postexilic J writer, proposing that the preponderance of 'elohim in this chapter "is probably governed by the fact that Jethro is a foreigner" (The Life of Moses: The Yahwist as Historian in Exodus–Numbers [Louisville: Westminster/John Knox, 1994], 209). Many, like Van Seters, question the existence of an E source (cf. G. I. Davies, "Introduction to the Pentateuch," in The Pentateuch, ed. John Barton and John Muddiman, Oxford Bible Commentary [Oxford: Oxford University, 2001], 27; for a good summary of the arguments, cf. Robert Gnuse, "Redefining the Elohist," JBL 119 [2000]: 201–20). Certainly, the alleged E traditions are widely scattered and lack any sense of a coherent plot. Still, the evidence does suggest that old northern traditions have been preserved in the Pentateuch, expressing a terminology and theology and presuming a social setting, also witnessed in the prophets Hosea, Micah, and Jeremiah but most fulsomely expressed in the book of Deuteronomy (cf. Stephen L. Cook, The Social Roots of Biblical Yahwism , SBLStBL 8 [Atlanta: Society of Biblical Literature, 2004], 231–44). Indeed David M. Carr, who rejects the idea of an E "source," nonetheless proposes that preexilic northern traditions were given a "later Southern extension" in the formation of Genesis, specifically (Reading the Fractures of Genesis: Historical and Literary Approaches [Louisville: Westminster John Knox, 1996], 150–51). Alternatively, we may think of E not as an independent documentary source but as a northern editing of the old J epic, with inserts and expansions preserving northern traditions and ideals.

5. In 18:11, the Name is necessary to distinguish the LORD from other gods: "Now I know that the LORD is greater than all gods [*kol-ha'elohim*], because he delivered the people from the Egyptians." Exod 18:1 and 8-10 also recall the deliverance from Egypt, calling the Name particularly to mind.

6. In Num 10:29 and Judg 4:11, Moses's father-in-law is called Hobab. Num 10:29, which also says that Hobab was the son of Reuel, may represent an attempt to consolidate these traditions.

7. St. John Chrysostom wrote, "For nothing was more humble than he, who being the leader of so great a people, and having overwhelmed in the sea the king and the host of all the Egyptians, as if they had been flies, and having wrought so many wonders both in Egypt and by the Red Sea and in the wilderness, and received such high testimony, yet felt exactly as if he had been an ordinary person. As a son-in-law he was humbler than his father-in-law; Moses took advice from him and was not indignant" ("Homilies on 1 Corinthians 1.4," cited in *The Ancient*

Christian Commentary on Scripture, vol. 3, ed. Joseph T. Lienhard; gen ed. Thomas Oden [Downers Grove, IL: Intervarsity, 2001], 94).

8. This mountain is called both Horeb and Sinai in Scripture. "Horeb" does not appear at all in the New Testament and is found seventeen times in the Hebrew Bible. Three are E traditions concerning the exodus: Exod 3:1; 17:6; 33:6. By far the majority of references (nine) come from Deuteronomy, a book couched as Moses's last words to the people before their entry into the land, which emphasizes Moses over Aaron and the priestly calling of "the whole tribe of Levi" over the claims of Aaron's line (see Deut 18:1). Another two (1 Kgs 8:9 [quoted in 2 Chr 5:10] and 19:8) come from the Deuteronomistic History in Joshua, Judges, Samuel, and Kings, built on Deuteronomy's idea of covenant. The remaining two references also seem related to Deuteronomy or to the northern Levitical perspective Deuteronomy represents. So Psalm 106 (Horeb is mentioned in Ps 106:19) is a retelling of the exodus story similar to Deuteronomy 1–4, while Malachi (see Mal 4:4) emphasizes the Levitical priesthood (see Mal 2:4-9). The "Horeb" traditions, in short, seem to reflect northern Levitical ideas about Israel, priesthood, and God. "Sinai," of course, is the dominant term for the mountain where Moses received the Law. It appears forty times in the Bible, including four references in the New Testament (Acts 7:30, 38; Gal 4:24-25). In the Pentateuch, Sinai is mentioned thirteen times in Exodus, five times in Leviticus, and twelve times in Numbers, all in material associated with old southern priestly traditions emphasizing Aaron. The references to Sinai in Deuteronomy 33:2, 16 and Judges 5:5 are the exceptions that prove the rule: neither Deuteronomy 33 (Moses's final blessing on the tribes) nor Judges 5 (the Song of Deborah) was written for its context. Rather, both are ancient poems, incorporated into the books in which they appear (cf. William M. Schniedewind, *A Social History of Hebrew: Its Origins Through the Rabbinic Period* [New Haven: Yale University, 2013], 70–72).

9. Note that only one son is mentioned in Exod 2:22, but cf. 4:20.

10. In Exod 4:20, by contrast, Moses's wife and sons go with him back to Egypt.

11. Frank Moore Cross, "The Priestly Houses of Early Israel," in *Canaanite Myth and Hebrew Epic: Essays in the History of the Religion of Israel* (Cambridge: Harvard University, 1973), 195–215; Steven S. Tuell, "Excursus: Priests and Levites," in *1 and 2 Chronicles*; Interpretation (Louisville: Westminster-John Knox, 2001), 61–63; Steven S. Tuell, "The Priesthood of the 'Foreigner': Evidence of Competing Polities in Ezekiel 44:1-14 and Isaiah 56:1-8," in *Constituting the Community: Studies on the Polity of Ancient Israel in Honor of S. Dean McBride, Jr.*, ed. John T. Strong and Steven Tuell (Winona Lake, IN: Eisenbrauns, 2005), 183–204.

12. Many early Jewish and Christian interpretations wrestle with this inclusion and can only accept Jethro's role by seeing his confession in Exod 18:10-11 as a conversion. In Targum Pseudo-Jonathan of Exod 18:6, Jethro tells Moses that he has come in order to convert (Aramaic *l'tgyyr*); cf. *Exod Rab* 1:32; *Tankha* Buber *Yitro*, 5 (cited by Tigay, "Exodus: Introduction and Notes," 134); and *Mekhilta* (https://www.sefaria.org/Mekhilta_d'Rabbi_Yishmael.18.12.2?lang=bi; cited by

Childs, *Book of Exodus*, 333; and J. Coert Rylaarsdam, "The Book of Exodus: Introduction and Exegesis," in *The Interpreter's Bible*, vol. 1, gen. ed. George Arthur Buttrick [Nashville: Abingdon, 1952], 964). Among Christian interpreters, Cyril of Alexandria and the Venerable Bede (cited by Childs, 332) also see this scene as Jethro's conversion. On the other hand, Josephus notes that Moses did not "conceal the invention of this method; nor pretend to it himself: but informed the multitude who it was that invented it. Nay he has named Raguel [alternate spelling of Reuel {cf. Num 10:29, KJV}; i.e., Jethro] in the Books he wrote, as the person who invented this ordering of the people" (*Ant* III. 4.2; http://penelope.uchicago.edu/josephus/ant-3.html), giving due praise to a Gentile! Similarly, Augustine wrote that "Moses very prudently and humbly yielded to the advice of his father-in-law, foreigner though he was . . . . For he realized that from whatever intellect right counsel proceeded, it should be attributed not to him who conceived it but to the One who is truth, the immutable God" (*On Christian Teaching*, Prologue 7; cited by Lienhard, *Ancient Christian Commentary*, 94).

13. Exod 18 is paralleled in the selection of seventy elders in Num 11:11-17 (according to *Who Wrote the Bible?* 252, also E), and in Deut 1:9-18 (Walter Houston, "Exodus," in *The Pentateuch*, ed. Barton and Muddiman, 109; Carr, *Reading the Fractures of Genesis*, 30–31). As both of these passages place this tradition *after* Sinai, rather than before, Jewish commentators Rashi, ibn Ezra, and the Rashbam (cited by Propp, *Exodus 1–18*, 628; cf. also Childs, *Book of Exodus*, 321) suggest that ch. 18 too originally belonged in that setting. Some modern scholars have also proposed that the Exod 18 account has been moved (Durham, *Exodus*, 242; Van Seters, *Life of Moses*, ß 209 n. 3; *contra* Propp, 627–28). Walter Brueggemann ("Exodus," in *The New Interpreter's Bible*, vol. 1, gen. ed. Leander Keck [Nashville: Abingdon, 1994], 824) observes that the passage does seem somewhat intrusive in its current setting but concludes, "Likely chapter 18 is an independent tradition that insisted upon inclusion in the larger narrative." Note, however, that a common feature of the final form of the wilderness narrative is the placement of parallel traditions on opposite sides of Sinai: e.g., the manna and quail in Exod 16 and Num 11, water from the rock in Exod 17 and Num 20. Further, as Childs notes, Exod 18 "functions as a concluding scene . . . . Just for a moment, the writer pauses in the story to look backward and rejoice. The writer achieves his effect by slowing the pace of his narrative" (Childs, 327).

14. Cf. the genealogy of the priests of Dan in Judg 18:30. In the MT of this passage, in both the Leningrad and Aleppo Codices, scribes apparently offended by this claim have inserted a superscripted letter *nun* into the name "Moses" (*msh*; cf. LXX and the Vulgate), changing it to "Manasseh" (*m{n}sh*; cf. Judg 18:30, KJV)! For more evidence regarding a northern, Levitical, Mushite (rather than Aaronide) priesthood, cf. Cross, "Priestly Houses," 197–206.

15. As Terence E. Fretheim observes, the family connection is stressed in this chapter, where Jethro is called Moses's father-in-law (Hebrew *khoten*) thirteen times (18:1, 2, 5, 6, 7, 8, 12 [twice], 14, 15, 17, 24, 27) and a priest only once (18:1; cf. Fretheim, *Exodus*, Interpretation [Louisville: John Knox, 1991], 195). Propp

(*Exodus 1–18*, 635) pithily notes, "It is a common literary theme, and perhaps the truth, that those best able to govern society are the worst stewards of their own affairs. And it is equally a truism that one's in-laws are liable to point this out."

16. Palmer, *Let Your Life Speak*, 88.

17. John Wesley, "Rules of the Bands," 1744; cited in *John Wesley*, ed. Albert C. Outler, Library of Protestant Thought (New York: Oxford, 1964), 180.

18. Brueggemann ("Exodus," 829) observes that the two parts of this chapter could be called "the celebration of justice" (vv. 1-12) and "the institutionalization of justice" (vv. 13-27). This juxtaposition is more than incidental: "this liberated community must develop institutions that will sustain and stabilize the exodus vision in daily social practice."

19. Purves, *Crucifixion of Ministry*, 11.

20. Ibid., 9–10.

21. Ibid., 11.

22. Ibid.

23. Owens, "Staying with God," 131–32.

24. Ibid., 132.

25. *Pirkei Avot* 1:6; see https://www.sefaria.org/Pirkei_Avot.1.6?lang=bi&with=all&lang2=en.

26. Many commentators (e.g., Childs, 332; Fretheim, 199; Durham, 252) seem to assume that Jethro's statement "and God so commands it" (Exod 18:23) is an assertion: God *does* command it; the only question is whether Moses will indeed accept it. However, the verse does begin with the conditional particle *'im* ("if"), which may control not just the first statement ("if you do this") but also the second (implicitly, "[if] God so commands it"). In that case, Jethro's advice would be proffered humbly, trusting Moses's own discernment of God's will. Moses's prompt action would then be an indication that Moses *did* indeed discern this to be God's will.

27. Houston, "Exodus," 110.

Chapter 4 — Winded Prophet

1. David Kinnaman, *Faith for Exiles: 5 Ways for a New Generation to Follow Jesus in Digital Babylon* (Grand Rapids, MI: Baker, 2019), 19.

2. "Solitude Creates Space for God," *Henri Nouwen Society*, 24 April 2024, https://henrinouwen.org/meditation/solitude-creates-space-for-god.

3. For example, 1 Timothy 4:7.

4. Dallas Willard, *The Spirit of the Disciplines: Understanding How God Changes Lives* (New York: HarperOne, 1999), 14.

Chapter 5 — How "Ineffeciency: with God Prevents Pastoral Burnout

1. In Sebastian Traeger, Greg D. Gilbert, and David Platt, *The Gospel at Work: How the Gospel Gives New Purpose and Meaning to Our Jobs* (Grand Rapids: Zondervan, 2018), 18.

2. Christopher Ash, *Zeal without Burnout: Seven Keys to Lifelong Ministry of Sustainable Sacrifice* (The Good Book Company, 2016), 14.

3. Makoto Fujimura, *Art and Faith* (Yale University Press, 2021), 18.

4. David Mathis, *Habits of Grace: Enjoying Jesus through the Spiritual Disciplines* (Wheaton, IL: Crossway, 2016), 142.

5. Fujimura, *Art and Faith*, 16.

Chapter 6 — Clergy Burnout, the Spirit's Fire, and Preaching

1. Jean Corbon, O.P., *The Wellspring of Worship*, trans. Matthew J. O'Connell (San Francisco: Ignatius, 1988), 7.

2. Rowan Williams, *Why Study the Past? The Quest for the Historical Church* (Grand Rapids: Eerdmans, 2005), 93.

3. Rowan Williams, *On Christian Theology* (Oxford: Blackwell, 2000), 146–47.

4. Here I am following the discussion in Veli-Matti Kärkkäinen, *Christ and Reconciliation: A Constructive Christian Theology for the Pluralistic World*, vol. 1 (Grand Rapids: Eerdmans, 2013), 368–72.

5. On God's "disarming beauty" see Julian Carron, *Disarming Beauty: Essays on Faith, Truth, and Freedom* (Notre Dame: University of Notre Dame Press, 2017).

6. Lesslie Newbigin, *Foolishness to the Greeks: The Gospel and Western Culture* (Grand Rapids: Eerdmans, 1986), 124.

7. Bryan D. Spinks, *The Worship Mall: Contemporary Responses to Contemporary Culture* (New York: Church Publishing, 2010), 216.

8. Here I have benefitted from the insight of Mark A. McIntosh, *Divine Teaching: An Introduction to Christian Theology* (Oxford: Blackwell, 2008), 187.

9. Pope Francis, *The Joy of the Gospel (Evangelii Gaudium): Apostolic Exhortation*, United States Conference of Catholic Bishops, Washington, DC (Vatican City: Libereria Editrice Vaticana, 2013), 6.

Chapter 7 — Comfort-curated Ministry

1. C. S. Lewis, *The Screwtape Letters* (New York: Harper, 2002), 233.

2. Purves, *Crucifixion of Ministry*, 13.

3. Adrian Plass, *A Smile on the Face of God* (London: Hodder and Stoughton, 1990), 189.

4. Burgess, Andrews, and Small, *A Pastoral Rule for Today* (IVP Academic, 2019).

5. In Frederick Buechner, *Wishful Thinking* (Harper San Francisco, 1973).

Chapter 8 — The Work of Rest

1. Portions of this article were first published in Stephen L. Woodworth, *I begot you: Reimagining the father metaphor for Pastoral Ministry in the twenty-first century*, doctoral dissertation, Gordon-Conwell Theological Seminary, 2012.

2. Saint Gregory the Great, *The Book of Pastoral Rule*, in Nicene and Post Nicene Fathers, ed. Phillip Schaff and Henry Wace, vol. 12 (Peabody, MA: Hendrickson, 1995), B1.

3. Richard Baxter, *The Reformed Pastor: A Discourse on the Pastoral Office*, ed. Samuel Parker (William Baynes, uncopyrighted, 1808). The phrase "showing the nature of the pastoral work" first appeared as part of the title of the book in the 1657 edition.

4. For a comprehensive overview of changes in pastoral identity, see H. Richard Niebuhr and Daniel Williams, eds., *The Ministry in Historical Perspectives* (New York: Harper and Brothers, 1956).

5. William H Willimon, *Pastor: The Theology and Practice of Ordained Ministry* (Nashville, TN: Abingdon, 2002), 12.

6. David Fisher, *The 21st Century Pastor: A Vision Based on the Ministry of Paul* (Grand Rapids, MI: Zondervan, 1996), 24.

7. John Johnson, "Seeking Pastoral Identity," *The Spurgeon Fellowship Journal* (Fall 2007): 1.

8. James M. Gustafson, "The Clergy in the United States," in *Professions in America*, ed. Kenneth Lynn (Boston, MA: Beacon, 1967), 70.

9. Eugene Peterson, *The Contemplative Pastor: Returning to the Art of Spiritual Direction* (Grand Rapids, MI: Eerdmans, 1989), 15.

10. Thomas C. Oden, *Pastoral Theology: Essentials of Ministry* (New York: HarperCollins, 1983), 5.

11. Brian Williams, *The Potter's Rib: Mentoring for Pastoral Formation* (Vancouver, British Columbia: Regent College, 2005), 21–22.

12. Joe E. Trull and James E. Carter, *Ministerial Ethics: Being a Good Minister in a Not-So-Good World* (Grand Rapids, MI: Baker Academic, 2004), 25.

13. Marva Dawn and Eugene Peterson, *The Unnecessary Pastor* (Grand Rapids, MI: Eerdmans, 2000), 4.

14. Cf. Fritz Kling, *The Meeting of the Waters: 7 Global Currents that Will Propel the Future Church* (Colorado Springs, CO: David C. Cook, 2010).

15. David A. Steele, *Images of Leadership and Authority for the Church: Biblical Principles and Secular Models* (New York: University Press of America, 1986), xi.

16. Richard John Neuhaus, *Freedom for Ministry: A Critical Affirmation of the Church and Its Mission* (New York: Harper and Row, 1979), 35.

17. Trull and Carter, *Ministerial Ethics*, 21–22.

18. Jeff Iorg lists "security" as the second most important character quality of pastors after integrity (*The Character of Leadership* [Nashville, TN: Broadman and Holman, 2007], 47).

19. Fisher, *21st Century Pastor*, 20, 23.

20. Peterson, *Contemplative Pastor*, 18.

21. Ibid., 17.

22. Watchman Nee, *Sit, Walk, Stand: The Process of Christian Maturity* (Carol Stream, IL: Tyndale House, 1977), 2.

23. Eugene Peterson, *Working the Angles* (Grand Rapids, MI: Eerdmans, 1993), 67–69.

Chapter 9 — Confronting the Myth of the Balanced Life

1. Tom Rath, *StrengthsFinder 2.0* (New York: Gallup, 2007), 37.

2. Ibid.

3. Wayne Cordeiro, *Leading on Empty: Refilling Your Tank and Renewing Your Passion* (Minneapolis, MN: Bethany House, 2009), 25–26.

Chapter 11 — Time Alone: Discovering My Identity

1. Bruce Demarest, *Satisfy Your Soul: Restoring the Heart of Christian Spirituality* (Colorado Springs: NavPress, 1999), 94–95.

2. Henri Nouwen, *The Only Necessary Thing: Living a Prayerful Life* (New York: The Crossroad Publishing Company, 1999), 42.

3. Ruth Haley Barton, *Sacred Rhythms: Arranging Our Lives for Spiritual Transformation* (Downers Grove, IL: InterVarsity, 2006), 31.

4. Stephen W. Smith, *Soul Custody: Choosing to Care for the One and Only You* (Colorado Springs: David C. Cook, 2010), 52.

5. Henri Nouwen, *In the Name of Jesus: Reflections on Christian Leadership* (Chestnut Ridge, NJ: The Crossroads Publishing Company, 1996), 18.

6. Ibid., 22.

7. Ibid., 38.

8. Ibid., 39.

9. Richard Rohr, *Everything Belongs: The Gift of Contemplative Prayer* (Chestnut Ridge, NJ: The Crossroads Publishing Company, 1999), 82.

10. M. Basil Pennington, *True Self, False Self: Unmasking the Self Within* (New York: The Crossroad Publishing Company, 2000), 46.

11. Peter Scazzero, *Emotionally Healthy Spirituality: It's Impossible to Be Spiritually Mature, While Remaining Emotionally Immature* (Franklin, TN: Integrity, 2006), 80.

12. Nouwen, *The Only Necessary Thing*, 42.

13. Siang-Yang Tan and Douglas Gregg, *Disciplines of the Holy Spirit: How to Connect to the Spirit's Power and Presence* (Grand Rapids: Zondervan, 1997), 47.

14. Dallas Willard, *The Spirit of the Disciplines: Understanding How God Changes Lives* (San Francisco: Harper and Row, 1988), 161.

15. Henri Nouwen, *The Way of the Heart: Connecting with God through Prayer, Wisdom, and Silence* (New York: Ballantine, 1981), 15, 18.

www.ingramcontent.com/pod-product-compliance
Lightning Source LLC
Chambersburg PA
CBHW071125090426
42736CB00012B/2013